CHRISTIANITY AND THE FRENCH REVOLUTION

CHRISTIANITY
AND THE
FRENCH REVOLUTION

By A. AULARD

Translated by Lady Frazer

NEW YORK

Howard Fertig

1966

First published in English by Ernest Benn Limited,
London in 1927

HOWARD FERTIG, INC. EDITION 1966

Published by arrangement with Ernest Benn Limited

Library of Congress Catalog Card number: 66-24341

PRINTED IN THE UNITED STATES OF AMERICA
BY NOBLE OFFSET PRINTERS

TRANSLATOR'S NOTE

A FEW explanations about the Republican Calendar of the French Revolution may prove useful to readers of this book.

The Republican Calendar started its Year I. on the 22nd September 1792, the day of the Autumn Equinox and the date of the proclamation of the Republic.

The year was divided into twelve months, each month having three uniform decades. The tenth day, called *Décadi*, was to be the day of rest; thus the old week and the old Sunday were ruled out.

But twelve months of thirty days each make only 360 days; thus in ordinary years five extra days, and in leap years six extra days, had to be intercalated. These complementary days bore the name of *sans-culottides*.

The feasts and names of saints in the Gregorian Calendar had also to go by the board, and for these the names of plants, metals, animals and agricultural implements were substituted. The invention of such a confusing calendar is due to the conventionel, Gilbert Rome. The new style came to a sudden end in the Year XIII., after lasting less than fourteen years; for, after starting on 22nd September 1792, it gave way again to the old Gregorian Calendar on 31st December 1805.

The famous mathematician Laplace, who was also a senator, induced the French Senate, on the 21st Fructidor, the last month of the Republican year, in the Year XIII., to restore the old Gregorian Calendar to its familiar place.

Fructidor corresponds to our August. The poetic

nomenclature of the months in the Republican Calendar was furnished by the comic poet Fabre d'Eglantine, who died on the scaffold :

Vendémiaire	corresponds	approximately to	September.
Brumaire	,,	,,	October.
Frimaire	,,	,,	November.
Nivôse	,,	,,	December.
Pluviôse	,,	,,	January.
Ventôse	,,	,,	February.
Germinal	,,	,,	March.
Floréal	,,	,,	April.
Prairial	,,	,,	May.
Messidor	,,	,,	June.
Thermidor	,,	,,	July.
Fructidor	,,	,,	August.

PREFACE

During the French Revolution Christian religion incurred serious danger; the shock of violence caused it to totter, and the ground might have been cut from under its feet had the storm of fury been free to persist.

A dechristianization of France started in 1793, and in the Year II., first with the Cult of Reason, then with that of the Supreme Being. To defend the country and the Revolution was the foremost aim against the priests, who showed themselves hostile. It seemed as if the priesthood was indestructible except by the overthrow of its altars. That work was carried out by revolutionary patriotism, and supported by a movement of free-thought, which had long been bred through the intolerance of the State religion, while philosophers like Voltaire stimulated and disseminated it. Throughout the greater part of the country the illiterate peasantry allowed things to take their own course, and this indifference almost suggests that these masses had never been thoroughly christianized. It is a startling fact that the closing of churches and their desecration had not occasioned serious riots like those which shortly before had broken out through the persistence of some feudal rights under the Revolution. Supposing the success of the National Defence had been delayed, and a victory, a liberating victory, such as that of Fleurus, had been delayed even by a few months, it is a question whether the protracted Terror, considered as a dechristianizing factor, would not have dealt the death-blow to the Catholic religion in particular, nay, to Christianity in general.

PREFACE

Not long ago, in specialized writings, I expressed a rather different opinion. It seemed to me then that Christianity was indestructibly rooted in the soul of the French. Since then, having read more documents, and now having perhaps a clearer insight into the facts as a whole, I am startled at the ease with which the people of France in 1794 began to drop their customary worship.

The peril thus run by Christianity at the time of the Worship of Reason and the Worship of the Supreme Being is the most outstanding episode in the religious history of the French Revolution.

It was preceded by the contrary attempt to link the Gallican Church more closely to the State by means of the Civil Constitution of the Clergy, followed by an attempt at liberty and laicizing the Church. This was the era of the Separation of Church and State, which lasted for seven years, and to which the Concordat put an end. Such is the story which I wish to tell as briefly as possible, confining myself to essential facts and placing them in their mutual relation.

When I speak of Christianity I refer chiefly to Catholicism, but the two French Protestant Churches, the Lutheran and the Calvinistic, were also affected by the anti-religious movement of 1793 and that of the Year II.; hence it was the whole of Christianity which was involved, and that at a solemn hour, when a New France was being called into existence.

The bibliography of such a subject is immense. I have numerous predecessors.[1] A volume larger than this one

[1] The most famous of these predecessors, Edgar Quinet, has, as a matter of fact, published a book with the same title as mine: but he put himself specially at a philosopher's point of view. I put myself at the historical point of view, for I am telling a tale.

would be needed to enumerate books, collections and authors, even if only the most important ones were mentioned. I have given as references many sources in various earlier writings of mine where I have dealt at length with some parts of a subject of which I treat to-day as a whole —*e.g.* in my *Political History of the French Revolution*, in my *Études et Leçons* (second and fifth series), in my book, *Le Culte de la Raison et le Culte de l'Être suprême*. I have drawn principally on the laws, and the large collections of texts and contemporary documents, whether published or unpublished. I could not read all these records, but only those which a man can read in the space of his lifetime. Yet there are some writings of our own period which have been of great service to me, such as the interesting doctoral dissertation of the Abbé Giraud on the "Religious History of the Department of the Sarthe" during the Revolution, and the instructive history of the small town of Beaumont-du-Périgord, by L. Testut: in both I have found evidence of value as to the religious faith of the peasants in two regions of France. I also have drawn information from the accurate monographs of Armand Lods on the Protestant Churches during the Revolution.

My endeavour has been to be impartial. I think I have been so. I have tried my best to avoid hypotheses, rash generalizations and too absolute assertions—a difficult task when the case in point is religion.

A. Aulard.

CONTENTS

CHAPTER II.—*continued*

CHAPTER IV.—*continued*

CHAPTER I

CHAPTER I

CHRISTIANITY AT THE END OF THE OLD RÉGIME AND THE OPENING OF THE REVOLUTION

§ I

Catholicism as State religion; old toleration of the Jews; recent toleration of Protestants

TOWARDS the end of the old régime, and at the opening of the Revolution, Christianity seemed flourishing in France.

The Catholic, Apostolic and Roman religion was the ruling one. It was the religion of a king styled the *very Christian King*. It was the religion of a nation which the popes called the *Elder Daughter of the Church*. The French people were supposed to have only a single and identical religion—namely, the Catholic one. That religious unity for which Louis XIV. and Louis XV. had so strenuously laboured seemed realized; and it was not a mere appearance, since there were very few non-Christian Frenchmen and the non-Catholics were not very numerous.

The non-Christians were the Jews; they were tolerated, and they formed groups established in the south-west, in the east and in Paris, while individually they were found here and there in many towns. But their existence did not impair the religious unity of the kingdom, for the reason that they were hardly reckoned as Frenchmen. They made no propaganda; they were not popular; no Catholic is noted as having left his own faith to become a Jew. The popes did not fear the Israelite religion; they had even befriended, at Carpentras, a Jewish colony which had swarmed into France.

As for the Gallican Church, the great danger of the Protestant schism seemed averted; the revocation of the Edict of Nantes, the large emigration of Calvinists, and the system of Terror continued by Louis XV. united to secure the benefit of the Catholic Church.

Yet there was something altered on the eve of the Revolution. Since the edict of November 1787 it was allowable to call oneself a Protestant, and a sort of civil status was granted to non-Catholics. But Protestants had not acquired full freedom of conscience; they were not allowed to conduct their worship publicly; and their heresy was officially considered as a disgrace to be concealed while it was tolerated, or rather to be tolerated while it was concealed. The unity of the Gallican Church was seemingly not affected by it.

What was the number of French Calvinists at that period? There are no trustworthy records. Voltaire speaks of one hundred thousand families; Condorcet of a million individuals; others of five to six hundred thousand.

This latter figure must come close to the fact, though exceeding it a little—for an official census in 1802 gives a total of 479,312 Protestants in the territory of Old France. The Protestants dwelt mostly in the south and west, where formerly they had dominated. There were some of them in the big cities, especially in Paris. They included few peasants and few artisans: Protestants formed an élite of intelligence and wealth.

They were much valued in the intellectual society

which to-day we would term liberal; in circles where the writings of the "philosophers" were read—where, consciously or the reverse, a revolution was brewing—they were, one may say, esteemed not only as martyrs, as victims of despotism, but as guardians of the true evangelical morality, or as a kind of rationalistic Christians; and it looked as if to favour Protestants constituted one of the means to fight, or to restrain, the despotism of the Church.

These feelings had penetrated even the royal policy. It is notable, and a sign of the period, that twice over Louis XVI. had placed at the head of his Government a Calvinist, Necker. No doubt if Necker had been a Frenchman his Calvinism would have seemed objectionable in a Prime Minister. As he was a foreigner, and from Geneva, at a period when patriotism was not as exclusive as it is at present, the fact of his being a Protestant was condoned. Yet the fact was obvious, but I do not find that the corporate clergy even protested when the King, in order to save his imperilled country, called thus on a heretic. As an object of popular enthusiasm, of course not as a heretic, but as an enemy, then as a victim, of despotism, Necker, by being in power, enhanced the prestige of Protestantism—yet without in any way impairing or shaking in the popular imagination the majestic outward pomp of the French Catholic unity.

There was one province of the kingdom, acquired hardly a century before, where liberty of thought reigned, and where under the royal sway heresy fraternized peacefully side by side—and sometimes in the same place of worship—with truth. That was Alsace, where about

220,000 Lutherans against 450,000 Catholics, according to the historian, Rodolphe Reuss, were entitled to exercise freely their worship, and in fact did exercise it thus, in spite of some petty vexations. But Alsace did not seem then to be as embodied in the personality of France as it became in 1790, when, at the federations, it spontaneously and freely pledged itself to the national pact.

This exception to the national unity was barely noticed; nowhere did that unity shine more resplendent than in the Gallican Church. That Church had formerly been agitated by rather noisy doctrinal quarrels. In 1789 Jansenism and the Bull Unigenitus were certainly not forgotten, yet they were hardly mentioned. Lay or clerical Jansenists still existed, but they remained silent. They had had the satisfaction of seeing their mortal enemies, the Jesuits, deprived by Louis XV. of the right to teach, and then suppressed, as a Society, by the Pope. Those quarrels were therefore hushed and the Church remained in unruffled unity.

§ II

Organization of the Gallican Church: her wealth, privileges and prestige

United and at peace, barely heeding the tolerance recently granted to the French Protestants (though complaining about it), disregarding the liberty still allowed to the Alsatian Protestants, the Gallican Church shone with the splendour of an unrivalled power.

Her prestige was not in any way weakened in the popular eyes by the fact that with reference to the royal power her clergy was divided into two groups : the *French* clergy and the so-called *foreign* clergy.

The French clergy was that of the provinces which had belonged to the kingdom in 1561, and which were represented at those "Assemblies of the Clergy" where the dues owing to the King were discussed under the name of "*don gratuit*"; there the authority, the importance, of that clergy were manifested by advice, petitions and remonstrances.

The foreign clergy was that of the provinces which had been united to France subsequently to the sixteenth century: Artois, Flandre, Hainaut, Alsace, Franche-Comté, Roussillon and Corsica. They had the same privileges as the French clergy, cherished the same sentiments and held the same attitude, both religious and political.

Though the popular opinion took no account of this geographical division, it drew the line in the Gallican Church between the seculars and the regulars, having greater regard for the former, and in the secular clergy it discriminated between the higher clergy, which was wealthy and haughty, and the lower clergy, which was poor and plain. Many bishops were patricians, many of the parish priests and curates were plebeians. Thus we see aristocratic tendencies in the high clergy and democratic ones in the inferior clergy. But the links binding the hierarchy were both solid and visible. The difference of opinion between the inferior clergy and the bishops or archbishops was merely a social and political one, not at all a religious one, and though some incumbents were dissatisfied with their bishops this great corporation, in its entirety, moved harmoniously.

As to the regular clergy, it was in decay. It was poorly recruited. We have no reliable statistics, but we have some figures of details. For example, the various orders of Benedictines had fallen from 6434 in 1770 to 4300 in 1790. There was a report of a general slackening of discipline and morals. A commission of regulars, formed of ecclesiastics and laymen, which worked from 1766 to 1780, raised the age for taking vows to twenty-one years for men and to eighteen for women. It suppressed nine orders but went no further. The decadence continued as well as the unpopularity, but it was a sort of vague—not a spiteful—unpopularity, which did not extend to all individuals. The Carthusian, Dom Gerle, is given a place of honour in a picture, *The Oath in the Tennis Court*, by the great painter David.

Notwithstanding this decadence of the regular clergy the Gallican Church, taken as a whole, made an impressive show.

Between the Pope and the King, between Versailles and Rome, the Gallican Church, formerly drawn in two by these two powers, now felt at anchor in a sort of independence. From the time when the Jesuits had to break off their activity, Ultramontanism was less militant, and the French clergy confined themselves to a moderate Gallicanism.

Thus on the eve of the Revolution the régime of the Concordat worked without serious difficulties and without grave incidents.

We have here an opulent Church unpaid by the State, living on her own wealth. She does not merely possess the tithes—a legal tax imposed for her exclusive benefit; not merely does she possess the offerings and alms of her flock; she owns important landed property, a part of the soil of France. What part? It has never been ascertained exactly. The clergy did not flaunt its wealth. Under the Constituent Assembly, when the State laid hands on Church property, only vague valuations were made. The Constituent Rabaut Saint-Étienne said that the Church owned one-fifth of the land and the Constituent Treilhard valued it at 4,000,000 livres. As to the amount of the income, the Constituents were unable to agree. Talleyrand estimated it at 150,000,000—70,000,000 for the proceeds of property and 80,000,000 for tithes. Treilhard valued it at over 200,000,000; Chasset at 303,000,000. All that was known was that the Church was very rich, and the notion of her wealth—whether exaggerated or not—added to the prestige of the Church on the eve of the Revolution.

It did not, however, enhance her popularity. The reproach against her was not so much that she was rich as that she used her wealth ill. The poverty of the lower clergy, of the priests who had the care of souls, shocked the people through its flagrant injustice, by contrast with the luxury of the high dignitaries, of the bishops and archbishops—a luxury sometimes outrageous. The Church property assigned to an ecclesiastic in virtue of his office was called a benefice. In many parishes the titulary of the benefice, often called *Curé primitif*, received the benefice in all its forms, tithe or stipend, without doing any duties. Another priest, vicar or curate, acted as *locum tenens*, with a stipend paid by the beneficiary, and that stipend was called *portion congrue*. In spite of several

Royal Acts, which fixed a minimum stipend—for example, of four hundred francs—it happened that many parsons remunerated by the *portion congrue* received a yearly income very inferior to that minimum, or even subsisted solely on the charity of their flock, and suffered want. These sufferings were not without their share in fostering a revolutionary spirit amongst the lower clergy. They explain in part not only the very success of the Revolution—a success which the lower clergy accelerated—but also indirectly the vicissitudes, nay, the grave peril, through which Christianity itself passed at that period.

Notwithstanding the unfair division of her revenue the Gallican Church drew, none the less, strength from her wealth. No doubt she did not dispose of it in full independence, since the King had the right to nominate to a number of regular or secular benefices. A churchman, a Crown functionary, acted as keeper for the King of what was called the *Feuille des bénéfices*, and by these nominations, which gave the King great influence, the State not only intervened in Church matters, but intervened to great effect.

On the other hand, as to the consistorial benefices—that is, those (bishoprics or abbeys) whose bulls or provisions were granted only after deliberation in the Consistory of Cardinals—the titularies had to pay to the Pope, under the name of *annates*, a due equal in principle to half the year's income. This contribution of pence to the Roman Court, to which the Revolution put an end, was most unpopular, and had always been so. The amount thus paid to the Pope was not high—perhaps 3,000,000 francs in 1789—but the payment went against the grain, and the dislike was, so to speak, national — nay, traditional. However, in spite of the State's interference in the administration of her wealth, and in spite of the subsidy exacted by the Pope, the Gallican Church was in possession of sufficient financial autonomy, as well as of sufficient wealth.

The greatness of the position which the clergy held at that period amid the people cannot be exaggerated. It occupied the very first rank and highest honour in the three estates. It enjoyed privileges for everything, and especially so as regards taxation. In principle it was entirely relieved of taxes, but it granted freely, or at least with a majestic semblance of liberty, a "gratuitous gift" to the King—a gift on which the clergy deliberated in its periodic general assemblies. It kept a general agent at the Court, who was a sort of minister without portfolio. That functionary alone kept all the registers of the Civil Status. The number and brilliance of the clergy's universities, the number and brilliance of its charitable works, all its wealth, all its privileges, all its influence, which was interwoven with all affairs, rendered the Gallican Church, especially when considered among the high clergy which led and represented it, a power alike strong and imposing.

§ III

Faith and incredulity

Did the Catholic religion, so splendidly represented by the Gallican Church, dwell strongly in the soul of the French people on the eve of the Revolution?

If we read Voltaire's writings, and if we recognize how successful they were, it is easy to see the waning of faith under Louis XV. and under Louis XVI. Almost the whole of polite society—the Court, the town, as it was called, all the intellectual and brilliant world which in the eyes of the foreigner personifies France—acclaimed the author of the *Pucelle*, and his scoffings, and applauded his abusive and amusing shafts of irony aimed against Christianity, against its dogmas, its ceremonies and its pastors.

Incredulity was displayed in scholarly circles. Young noblemen, such as the unfortunate Chevalier de la Barre, delighted in sacrilege, in the very middle of that century. Preachers from their pulpits, bishops in their mandates, ceaselessly denounced the progress of impiety. To be impious was to be in the fashion, and that fashion was followed by the nobility, especially by the Court nobles: a great lord who was pious, even a pious Bourbon, became an anomaly, and his piety aroused surprise.

This incredulity was not the work of philosophers—it was this incredulity which incited the philosophers to write thus against religion; of course they did so with pleasure and sincerity, but their daring would have been less had they not addressed themselves to such a stimulating and appreciative gallery. I do not know if the best society was more thoroughly irreligious under Louis XV. and Louis XVI. than under Louis XIV. Perhaps it may be called less impious, for one hears less about atheism and atheists. When one has read the sermons of Bossuet, the *Don Juan* of Molière, La Bruyère's chapter on religion, one can hardly believe that atheism was less current during the reign of the great King than during the period of Voltaire, whose philosophy was fashionable amongst well-bred men.

Even if we retrace French history to the very heart of the Middle Ages we shall not succeed in finding a period in which piety was general, solid, profound, embracing the whole both of the individual and of the nation. Always in France there has existed free and censorious satire. Occasionally this jeering incredulity finds expression at the very portals of cathedrals, in grotesque statues, just as it shows itself in the troubadour tales of the time and in its satirical literature.

At the period which we are studying France was chiefly a land of peasants. The bourgeois, the urban artisans, the scholars, were only few in comparison with the great mass of rustics—an illiterate mass.

Did religion hold sway in the hearts of the peasants during the reign of Louis XVI.? In those countrysides devoid of roads, of news, of the enlightenment peculiar to cities, had the peasants preserved what is styled their fathers' faith? Had they kept it intact and ardent? It is necessary to put this question, and to try to answer it, if we wish to know what were in the rural districts the chances of success for the great dechristianizing attempt at the time of the Terror.

It is not easy to answer the question.

First of all, before we ask ourselves whether the faith of the French peasant had declined on the eve of the Revolution, it is well to ask ourselves if their ancestors had ever been christianized, in the full and true sense of the word.

When Christianity spread in Gaul, when it moved from the cities to the country, did it effect in the rural world one of those conversions which renew the whole man? Or did it only to a small extent, artificially and externally, overlay those beliefs of the period which it dubbed superstitions? With all the care which the preachers took to make use of local customs, changing little more than their names, did the French peasant feel that his religion was a new one? Was he truly and deeply altered by it?

Only a few years ago, in an out-of-the-way country place of central France, I took part in the funeral of a peasant whose mourners had to walk over three miles before they could reach the church and minister—four miles without a sign of Christianity—an hour and a half's slow march during which were exhibited rites and gestures obviously anterior to Christianity, and which those peasants performed unanimously, as through unconscious atavism.

I had that day the impression that in our rural districts far from towns (the one I mean is very remote) Christianity still fits badly into old beliefs, and assuredly has not entirely exterminated them.

I do not wish to generalize about an incident—an anecdote—even a true one, since I who speak witnessed it. I merely venture to ask myself whether, when we speak of the French peasant's faith, we speak of the true Christian faith, the faith of the Catechism in its original purity, or whether it is not blent with a strong infusion of still older beliefs.

§ IV

Example of the Department of the Sarthe

Whether pure or contaminated, that Christianity had entered into the habits of the peasantry. On a general and superficial view it is no exaggeration to say that in 1789 faith was more widely diffused, and more living, in the country than in the town.

That faith was due to habit, and friendship had its share in it. The peasant liked the lower clergy, those parish and officiating priests, those curates, with whom he lived on a footing of familiarity and who were as plebeian as he was himself. Many proofs of this friendship exist. The Abbé Giraud, author of a recent and very interesting dissertation on the *Religious History of the Department of the Sarthe from the Year* 1789 *to the Year IV.*, has studied and expounded this friendship in the diocese of Le Mans. The reasons he gives for it seem to be applicable to the whole of France. The clergy was popular because of its charity, of its intellectual culture, which in a world of ignorance shone brightly even when it was slender; then the schools knit the bond, though they were more numerous than good, and though the peasant as a rule could neither read nor write.

The importance and influence of the clergy in the rural districts were born also of the fact that the priests who celebrated births, marriages, deaths were both ministers of the cult and public functionaries. This combination of functions was so ingrained in the customs of the people that even when the civil status became laicized (through the law of the 20th September 1792) in the Department of the Sarthe the parish priests were chosen as Civil Status Officials up to the middle of the Year II.

Above all, the country priest was "the missionary of hygiene," the interpreter of official advice when epidemics were rampant, the man of "first aid" at a time when doctors were rare in rural parts.

The inhabitants of Le Mans are much attached to the ministers of religion.

The Abbé Giraud asks himself whether it is legitimate to infer from this that the population of the Department "was all but unanimous in practising the Catholic religion, in attending its offices and in observing its rules."

The word "communicants" used in taking a census of believers is vague, and does not indicate an actual practice.

M. Giraud collected the testimony of parish priests, both just before and during the Revolution, and many exceptions to the general practice of the faith may be seen in it. Thus the *curé* of Thoigné, in a memorandum on his district, said that long before 1792 some of his parishioners "had contracted the bad habit of going without the sacraments." The *curé* of Changé notes a minority who receive the sacraments only once a year, or not at all. In the town of Le Mans there are many abstentions. In Thermidor of the Year III. the Justice of the Peace of the Canton of Bessé notes that those who now frequent the services best are the very ones who absented themselves at the end of the old régime; and thus we learn that in 1789 there were people at Bessé who were not practising their religion.

In spite of all the laws against publicans, in country districts many inns were open and frequented during church-time. Lent was observed less and less. In his pastoral charge in 1789 the Bishop of Le Mans said: "Non-observance has become general. People who are not well off leave the observances of religion to the rich, the artisan leaves it to the man of leisure, the great man relies upon his rank and the rich upon his wealth to exempt himself. The abuse has reached such a pitch that it may be regarded as one of the plainest signs of the lowering of the moral standard in this kingdom. It is no good to look for Lent among us, it is no longer to be found."

Guilds were disappearing one by one. Even as far back as 1774 the parish priest of Changé notes that his parish guild has disappeared owing to the increase of drunkenness, irreligion and dancing."

...lls to the priesthood were becoming rarer in the ...e of Le Mans. At the beginning of the eighteenth ... the annual average of ordinations was forty- ...ing the years from 1784 to 1788 it was only

...em that on the eve of the Revolution there ... even in the country, a small minority of ... a large minority of indifferent people, ...ractice of religion was general, there ...tions, together with a sort of slack- ... the part of many of the faithful; ...enough faith to make an attempt ...impossible, but enough deeply ... an attempt very difficult or impossible unless circumstances disgusted people with their priests.

§ V

The attitude of the philosophers: Voltaire, Raynal

No one dreamed then, in 1789, of dechristianizing France.

Voltaire himself, who in his private letters used to talk of crushing *l'infâme*—that is, the Church—only wished for the present to destroy its despotic power. He believed that the people needed some religion, and might as well have that as any other so long as they remained ignorant, which meant for a very long time. This was also the opinion of Buffon and the philosophers. Rousseau, who called himself the enemy of the philosophers, only wanted to simplify Christianity and bring it back to its origins.

The philosophers did not openly demand either the alteration or the destruction of the Catholic religion, bu only that it should cease to be oppressive. They aske in the words of Montaigne in the sixteenth centu liberty of conscience. Or rather, they asked for it onl principle. Although they saw examples of the applic of this liberty in Holland, although it was actually tised in one province of the kingdom—namely, Alsac that they publicly asked for was toleration. What is tion? It is the attitude of religious truth when f error. Let us be kind and indulgent to the mist us not persecute or do them violence. That is t There is liberty of conscience when each indi an equal right to think what he likes, to practise his religion or none at all, the Government being neutral, a stranger to religion—in short, secular. This liberty was the evident result of eighteenth-century philosophy; but the philosophers were not asking for it—at least, not in so many words.

Voltaire did not for the present recommend the separation of Church and State. In a private letter he might extol the ideal time when the Government would concern itself no more with the worship of God than with cookery, but in a public writing he said: "Do you want your country to be powerful and peaceful? Then let religion be enjoined by the law of the State."

Religion must be purified and simplified, but above all we must have good priests, guardians of morality rather than theologians. It is the State alone which can and ought to effect this purification and simplification. Far from wishing to separate the Church from the State, the philosophers would desire to unite them more closely, so that the State might give laws to the Church. For them religion was a State affair.

One of the most influential and militant free-thinkers of the time was concealed beneath a cassock—I mean the Abbé Raynal. He wrote in 1780: "The State, it seems to me, is not made for religion, but religion is made for the State: that is the first principle. The general interest is the rule to determine everything that should exist in the State: that is the second principle. The people, or the supreme authority which is its depositary, alone has the right to judge whether any institution conforms to the general interest: that is the third principle. From these principles he inferred that the State has the right "to proscribe the established religion, to adopt a new one, or even to dispense with religion altogether, if it thinks fit." Raynal did not require the State to use this right, but he proclaimed it in order to tighten the bonds which united the Church to the State and to make them into a solid tie of subordination. He concluded: "The State is supreme in everything. The distinction between temporal power and spiritual power is a palpable absurdity; there can be and there ought to be only one single jurisdiction everywhere; it is for the public authority to command and to forbid."

Of all these philosophers Condorcet was the one who had most sense of the future, and he felt that separation meant the rule of liberty; in 1786 he wrote: "As public worship is necessarily the result of religious opinions about which a man's own conscience is the only lawful judge, it is evident that the expenses of public worship ought to be borne voluntarily by those who hold the opinions on which the worship is based." But he added: "It is none the less true that if a people are accustomed to see the expenses of public worship borne by public funds, and to receive instruction from the lips of priests, it is dangerous and even unjust to do violence to its habits by too hasty reforms, and this is a case where to act fairly and honestly we must wait till we have public opinion on our side."

We see then that even the bold pioneer Condorcet (who was not then a leader of opinion) was only in favour of the separation of Church and State in theory; he would postpone putting it into action indefinitely, and would be content to have a State religion, provisionally, for long enough.

What we call, by a neologism which dates from fifty years later, secularization was not unknown to the philosophers, but they were then not asking for the establishment of the secular system which the Convention ended by establishing.

§ VI

Religion as seen in the "Cahiers"

The lists (*cahiers*) of grievances and petitions which were drawn up by the Third Estate in 1789 were still less bold and exacting in religious matters.

I find in them only a few petitions for the reform or suppression of the religious orders, and a little Gallicanism here and there of a very moderate sort. Some complaints also occur about the wealth and luxury of the superior clergy. No great reform is asked for—not even the secularization of the civil status. Even religious toleration is seldom mentioned in the *cahiers* of the Third Estate. Only in the *cahier* of the Seneschal of Nîmes, drawn up no doubt under Protestant influence, have I found an express desire for liberty of thought, in these terms: "As to liberty of thought, nothing is worthier of the wisdom of His Majesty than to have permitted the free profession of any religion founded on sound morals, which is the only means of enlightening men and leading them to virtue; a work wisely begun by the edict of November 1787, and only waiting to be completed by the superior views of His Majesty and the progress of enlightenment in the nation." But elsewhere, when the Third Estate speaks of the edict in favour of Protestants, it is rather to ask that it should stop there, and that Catholicism should remain the sole religion of the State. Thus the Third Estate in the bailiwick of Sens proclaims its most firm attachment "to the Catholic, apostolic and Roman religion and to the exclusive maintenance of its worship throughout the kingdom, always excepting the observance of the King's declaration of November 1787 in favour of the non-Catholics." Even in Paris the Third Estate wishes nothing but civil toleration: "The Christian religion," it says, "enjoins civil toleration. Every citizen has the right to enjoy private liberty of conscience; public order does not permit of more than one dominant religion." In the bailiwick of Orleans there are many *cahiers* of the Third Estate which demand that the Catholic religion shall be dominant or even exclusive. The Third Estate of Chaigny demands that "complete silence be imposed on any sectarian who should dare to propose an impious toleration under the disguise of liberty, which sooner or later would be contrary to the peace of the nation and the welfare of its sovereign." "Let it be no longer permitted, Sire, to throw doubts upon your faith or upon the submission due to you. The Catholic religion is dominant in France; it was received in all the purity of its primitive maxims; it is the foundation of the liberties of the Gallican Church."

It may be affirmed that in the France of 1789 there were no more secularists than there were republicans. But a republican atmosphere was being created, although France had not yet thought of destroying the monarchy, and an atmosphere of free thought was likewise being formed, although the French had not yet thought of destroying religion, or even of modifying its doctrines; their one desire was to make its rule less despotic, and also to maintain what were called the liberties of the Gallican Church—that is, a relative independence of the Pope by means of a moderate Gallicanism.

CHAPTER II

CHAPTER II

THE CIVIL CONSTITUTION OF THE CLERGY, 1790-1792

§ I

The Revolution at first supported by the inferior clergy

THE Revolution set out with the support of the Catholic clergy—especially of the inferior clergy. This fact, sometimes forgotten, is too important not to be explicitly emphasized.

In the States-General at Versailles, when the Third Estate quarrelled with the two privileged Estates over the verification of *powers*, and the nobles, refusing to verify them together, formed a separate Chamber, the clergy did not wish to form a separate Chamber. They waited, they tacked about—they did not pronounce against the Third Estate nor against the revolutionary idea of the union of the orders—and finally, by a majority, and with acclamation, they took the side of the Third Estate, in favour of the Revolution.

Their position in all its stages was public, impressive and influential.

The first step was taken on 13th June 1789. The Third Estate, weary of vain discussion, decided to proceed by itself to the general verification of powers, by appealing in the first place to all the deputies. Only deputies belonging to the Third Estate had so far responded to this appeal when, on the 13th June, three parish priests of Poitou, called Lecesve, Ballard and Jallets, appeared to join them. They were received with a unanimous burst of gratitude, with an enthusiasm which became contagious. Fraternal sentiments were exchanged. The next day—the 14th—six more priests appeared, and at the same time it was said that a hundred priests had assembled apart from the Chamber of their Estate, and had decided to join them. The intrigues and underhand threats of the upper clergy alone prevented them from carrying out their decision at once. By patience and labour they obtained still better success, and at last, by a majority of some voices, their Estate voted for union. On the 22nd this majority in fact joined the Third Estate, with the support of several bishops, and having at their head Lefranc de Pompignan, Archbishop of Vienne (France). The Third Estate was now the National Assembly, and on that date they were joined by the majority of the clergy. President Bailly said, in his speech of welcome: "France will bless this memorable day; it will inscribe your name in the archives of the country." And the deputy Target, who was already fairly important, lauded "this day which Providence seems to desire to solemnize by converting the temple of religion into the temple of the fatherland."

The words were new, the sentiments were new: we behold the religion of the country all at once taking its place by the side of, or even above, the old religion of the State, precursor of a cult which was to give religious form to revolutionary patriotism, and which before a year was over was to have its altars in the federations. In the expression of their gratitude the patriots did not see that, while paying such honour to the ministers of religion, they were putting religion itself in the second place, nor did the ministers themselves perceive it in this new warm atmosphere of patriotism.

After the Royal session of 23rd June, when the Third Estate disobeyed the King, many of the clergy shared in their disobedience. On the 24th, when this act of disobedience was carried into effect, the majority of the clergy resumed their places in the National Assembly, and this courageous step was certainly not without its influence on the King, who seemed to approve of it, and on 27th June 1789 he definitely ordered the three Estates to unite.

At the opening of the Revolution then the inferior clergy walked hand in hand with the Third Estate. Their valuable and powerful assistance made everything easy to the Third. Without the parish priests the Revolution might have come to pass, but it would have come more slowly and in a different way. The revolutionists long cherished ardent gratitude to the priests, and the Catholic religion itself profited by this gratitude—which took the form of sustained deference and respect—and of the absence of anti-religious jokes in the "patriotic" newspapers and pamphlets of the time.

§ II

First political religious measures of the Constituent Assembly; tithes, Church property, Declaration of Rights, suppression of the religious orders

The Constituent Assembly refrained from handling religious matters during the year 1789, except in so far as they could do so without giving offence to the inferior clergy, who had deserved so well of the country.

The first attack on the constitution of the Gallican Church was made on the night of the 4th of August, by the decree which abolished in principle, and to some extent in practice, the feudal system and feudal rights. Article 5 of this decree, definitely formulated on 11th August, abolished all sorts of tithes and substitutes for tithes, but provided that they should be collected provisionally until the National Assembly should decide upon " some other means of providing for the expenses of Divine worship, for the sustenance of the ministers of the altar, the relief of the poor, the repairs and rebuilding of churches and presbyteries, and of all establishments, seminaries, schools, colleges, hospitals and communities to which they are now appropriated." Article 8 suppressed the occasional fees of country priests, but not until their stipends should be increased and pensions provided for the curates, while a special regulation was made to " fix the lot " of the town clergy. Article 12 prohibited the sending to Rome of money for " annates, or for any cause at all." Article 13 suppressed the privileges of bishops, archbishops, chapters, etc; and Article 14 forbade the holding of benefices in plurality if over the value of 3000 francs.

Displeasing as these measures were to the higher clergy and to the Pope, they were more than reassuring to the inferior clergy. At the same time, and in the same decree, striking homage was rendered to the Catholic religion under whose auspices the Revolution was placed, as the decree said, " for the welfare of France." The National Assembly ordered a medal to be struck and a *Te Deum* to be sung " by way of thanksgiving in all the parishes and churches of the kingdom." They begged the

King to allow this *Te Deum* to be sung in his chapel, in the presence of the Assembly.

The Catholic religion was, then, maintained by the Assembly, with solemn homage, in its pre-eminent place as the religion of the State, and the only national religion.

A few weeks later came the Declaration of the Rights of Man and of the citizen. The Assembly did not thereby proclaim that liberty of conscience which had always been condemned by the teaching of the Church, but merely toleration. The Article ran: "No one is to be molested for his opinions, even his religious opinions, provided that their manifestation does not disturb public order established by the law." These two words "even religious," show that the Assembly considered religious liberty as more dangerous than political liberty. Its language was rather that of toleration than of liberty; but it was a wide toleration, wider than that which had inspired the edict of 1787 in favour of the Protestants. These were no longer forbidden the public exercise of their worship, and in fact they began to exercise it almost publicly. That was more than the *Cahiers* had demanded. But on this point, as on so many others, the Assembly, hurried on by the pressure of events, and excited by strife, went further than the *Cahiers*, without going as far as the Revolution was to go eventually in the time of the Terror.

The clergy, upper and lower, made hardly any protest against this toleration—the width of which ought to have rendered them uneasy—and the desire for liberty was so strong that in this conflict a protest against any Article whatever of the Declaration of Rights would have excited public indignation.

The Act by which the Assembly in self-defence opened the era of religious warfare was the decree of 2nd November 1789, which, in order to avert the alarming financial crisis, declared that all Church property was at the disposal of the State. But it was careful to add that the State "would provide in a fitting manner for the expenses of public worship, the maintenance of the ministers and the relief of the poor."

To reassure the inferior clergy, and to retain their political support, the Assembly declared, by this same decree, that, "in the regulations to be made for the maintenance of the ministers of religion, it would be enacted that no living should be of less value than 1200 francs a year, besides house and garden." To the inferior clergy this opened a vista of real comfort compared with their present poverty. To the superior clergy it meant a reduction of income which would deprive them of their luxury and, as they thought, of their prestige. From that time onwards they set themselves almost as one body against the Revolution. It was then, especially when the decree of the 19th December 1789 ordered the sale of 400,000,000 livres of Church property (and Crown property), that the first germs of the civil political-religious war may be discovered which little by little brought first the new France and then the old religion to the verge of death.

§ III

Refusal to declare Catholicism the religion of the State

The Constituent Assembly treated the old religion as the religion of the State. But the further the Revolution progressed, and the more it applied the Rights of Man, the more illogical this treatment appeared.

This want of logic was evident when, on the 12th April 1790, Dom Gerle asked his colleagues of the Assembly to decree that "the Catholic, apostolic and Roman religion should be, and should always remain, the religion of the nation, and that its worship should be the only public and authorized one." This motion was so thoroughly in harmony with the *Cahiers* and with the gratitude felt by the Assembly towards the "patriotic" priests that it might have been passed in a fit of enthusiasm. But an adjournment was requested, which shows that there was a movemant of opinion towards the ideas which we now call secular; and "philosophy" scored a partial victory the next day—the 13th—when the Assembly substituted for the motion proposed by the Carthusian a sort of profession of Catholicism, in these terms: "The National Assembly, considering that it neither has nor can have any power over the conscience or over religious opinions, and that the majesty of religion and the profound respect due to it forbid its becoming a subject of discussion; considering that the attachment of the Assembly to the Catholic, apostolic and Roman religion cannot be called in question at a time when the expenses of this religion are being given the first place in the budget, and when, with a unanimous sentiment of respect, it has expressed its feelings in the only way befitting the dignity of religion and the character of the National Assembly; it decrees that it cannot, and ought not to, deliberate on the motion proposed, and that it will proceed with the order of the day concerning Church property." A large minority (of nearly 300 members) voted against this decree—that is, in favour of the motion of Dom Gerle.

This Assembly, which did not dare to refuse to declare the Catholic religion to be the religion of the State, and at the same time declared itself Catholic, seems to us to have taken a very little step on the way to secularization. The importance of the opposing minority shows us that this step seemed bold to contemporaries. Soon the minority raised a protest both against the sale of Church property and the rejection of Dom Gerle's motion. A part of the Gallican Church was beginning to call itself persecuted, not only because the nation was seizing its goods, but because its character as the State religion—the sole religion enjoying the privilege of public worship—was contested.

Other measures taken by the Assembly in ecclesiastical affairs, without causing so much emotion, had given cause for anxiety, as if religion was being attacked; these were the measures against the regular clergy. Here, too, going further than the *Cahiers*, the Assembly took up a bold position. It declared all vows suspended from 28th October 1789. The 13th of February 1790 was the date of the great decree on this subject: vows were not to be taken, all orders and congregations under vows were suppressed. Individuals were free to leave: a suitable pension was assigned to them (regulated by several other decrees). Those who refused, if males, were provided with houses to which they might retire. Nuns might remain where they were.

As to the secular congregations, the Assembly was besieged with motions about them—but it made no pronouncement.

The suppression of the regular clergy did not greatly disturb public opinion. But it turned many of these clergy into enemies of the Revolution.

§ IV

The Pope condemns the Declaration of Rights, in March 1790

What was the attitude of the Pope when confronted by this ecclesiastical policy of the Assembly? At first he was prudent and waited. Later on he seems to have feared a schism, to have been haunted by the remembrance of the English schism, somewhat as Louis XVI. was haunted at a later date by the tragic end of Charles I. He did not want to excite men's passions. If he lamented the decree of 4th August 1789, which suppressed the annates, he did not do it in public.

I would not attribute his animosity to the French Revolution merely to human and temporal motives. Nevertheless one must recognize that he quickly became very anxious, very dissatisfied with the affairs of Avignon and the Comtat-Venaissin. In the popular outbreaks which took place there, from the outset of the Revolution, Pius VI. saw, and rightly, the beginning of a movement which would end in reuniting to France these Papal possessions.

The Constituents, even if they had wanted to, could not give the Sovereign Pontiff any assurances on the subject without being false to their principles, because the inhabitants (or a majority of them), French in language and customs, desired to be reunited with the France of the Rights of Man. No such breach could be tolerated in the unification of the new country.

Plainly, the Pope could not be well disposed towards a Revolution which, though it might profess respect for religion and the Church, had taken, or was going to take, a kingdom from him.

On the 29th March 1790 the Pope took his stand firmly and clearly, though in the prudent form of a speech in a secret consistory, against the ecclesiastical policy of the Constituent Assembly, a policy which was attacking and disturbing religion and usurping the rights of the Apostolic See: *Per decreta quae a generalibus Nationis Comitiis prodierunt, ipsa impetitur perturbaturque Religio, hujus apostolicae Sedis usurpantur jura.*

Opposing doctrine to doctrine, he resolutely and directly attacked the very spirit of the French Revolution in the Declaration of the Rights of Man and of the citizen, which he condemned. To him the Article which declared the law to be the expression of the general will was dangerous, equally so the assertion that all citizens are entitled to take part in legislation either in person or through their representatives, because the implication is that no one is bound by laws to which he has not consented, *nec quemquam aliis obstringi legibus quam quibus ipse consentiat.* It was plain that, in the opinion of the Pope, the Declaration ruined the principle of authority, which is one of the foundations of the Church, and effaced the Divine origin of law. But his chief complaint was against the Article which stated that no one ought to be molested on account of his opinions—even his religious opinions. He blamed this Article, *quo libertas asseritur cogitandi, etiam de Religione, prout cuique libeat, suaque cogitata impune proferendi.* He was indignant that the question whether the Catholic religion should remain dominant (*dominatrix*) in the kingdom of France should be so much as discussed. He was angry that non-Catholics (*acathollici*) should be declared admissible to all employments, municipal, civil and military. He was angry that solemn monastic vows should not be maintained.

What was the Pope to do? He did not know to whom to turn in France for an authoritative expression of opinion. To the most Christian King? He had been deprived of his Royal authority and forced to sanction these decrees. To the bishops, the clergy? They were frightened and scattered. Nevertheless the Pope would not act without the advice of the clergy and of the King, for fear of provoking a schism. Then, raising his tone, he denounced the French nation which, acting "almost as a body and seduced by the image of an empty liberty, has meekly obeyed an assembly of philosophers who are biting and tearing one another. *Concilio philosophorum se invicem mordentium ac obtrectantium.*"

It was in this way that the Pope, now cautious and now threatening, set himself in opposition to the French Revolution, beginning from the month of March 1790.

§ V

The Civil Constitution: its essential characteristics, its spirit

The Pope knew that the Constituent Assembly was drafting a great law of ecclesiastical reform without his authority and in opposition to it.

It had appointed an "ecclesiastical committee" to prepare this law. Whether Jansenists or philosophers, all the members were Gallicans, of the old Royal type of Gallicanism, according to the four famous Articles voted by the Assembly of the clergy in 1682, to limit the authority of the Holy See and to strengthen that of the King. The ecclesiastical committee, with Camus and Duraud-Maillane, went back, as regards Gallicanism, to the policy of the *parlements*, which aimed at making the Church as subordinate to the State as possible and as free as possible from the authority of the Pope. Camus went quite as far as the Abbé Raynal as regards the power to be given to the State in religious matters. On the rostrum of the Constituent Assembly, in the sitting of the 1st June 1790, he declared: "We certainly have the power to alter religion." He added: "We shall not do it." But suggestions of this kind, publicly made and not contradicted, could not but shake the exclusive authority of the Catholic religion over the minds of men.

The Committee, however, had no intention of shaking this authority, nor above all did it intend to meddle with dogma. It called the "Constitution" which it proposed to give to the clergy "civil" on purpose to show that religion itself was not affected. The reporter, Martineau, made the most conservative statements. It was a question of "restoring to religion all its energy and dignity." "Institutions must be founded on the sacred basis of religion, on faith in a Supreme Being, the sovereign dispenser of good and ill, the avenger of crime and the source of virtue." He insisted: "It is to religion above all, gentlemen, that you have bound the success of your labours. Kings, subjects, magistrates—civil and military —you have required from all the solemn oath of fidelity to the nation, the law and the King, and that they should maintain with all their power the Constitution you have established. What have you done by this? You have proclaimed aloud to all that the salvation of the Empire is closely bound up with religion. For, without religion, an oath is but an empty word." The reforms proposed by the Ecclesiastical Committee "will consist merely in a return to the discipline of the early Church." The gist of it was—though the reporter did not use those words—the nationalization of the Catholic religion by means of a thorough Gallicanism—not the moderate sort of thing which appears in the *Cahiers*, and which was in 1789 that of most of the clergy.

After long debates, which cannot be summarized here, on 12th July 1790 the Constituent Assembly voted the measure for the Civil Constitution of the clergy.

This implied, to begin with, the rupture of the Concordat. The Assembly did not arrange this with the Pope. The King himself negotiated through his ambassador, M. de Bernis; the Assembly, however, took no notice of this negotiation, and the King sanctioned the Civil Constitution, on 24th August, before the negotiation was completed.

The main features of the Civil Constitution are as follows:

A return was made to the days before the Concordat, to the Pragmatic Sanction, in these terms: "Only one way of appointing to bishoprics and parishes will be recognized, and that is the method of elections." But the mode of election was much wider than in the time of the Pragmatic Sanction. Bishops were to be nominated by the electors of departments—the same electors who nominated the members of the departmental Assembly. Parish priests were to be nominated by the electors of the district—the same who nominated the members of the district Assembly. In this way non-Catholics were allowed to elect the ministers of the Catholic religion. The Abbé Grégoire proposed that only Catholics should vote. His amendment was rejected. But it was enacted that, for the election of a bishop and for that of parish priests, the voting should take place on a Sunday, "at the close of the parochial Mass which all the electors will be bound to attend."

In reality hardly anyone was excluded. The electoral assemblies for political or administrative elections took place in the churches; people often went to Mass before voting, whatever their persuasion was, and this homage paid to religion was so ingrained in their habits that no inference was to be drawn from it.

This order implied that every Frenchman was assumed to belong to the Catholic religion, and this assumption, which recalled the old régime, could not be very unpleasant to the clergy, and that was no doubt why they made but a feeble protest against the permission given to non-Catholics to take part in ecclesiastical elections with the help of a little pretence which everyone understood.

But the result of this same order that bishops and parish priests should be elected only by copyholders, that only citizens in active enjoyment of the franchise should take part in their election, excluded the poor, which was hardly in accord with current ideas about the restoration of the equality of " primitive " Christianity.

The one hundred and thirty-nine dioceses of the old régime, so unequal in extent, were reduced to eighty-three, one for each department; thus each department formed a diocese.

The bishop received canonical institution not from the Pope, but from another bishop called the Metropolitan, six of whom were created.

The number of the parish priests who were canonically instituted by the bishop was considerably reduced: communes of less than six thousand inhabitants might form only one parish and have one parish priest; but there was one to each commune.

The stipends of the clergy were provided by the State.

The Tithe Committee had arranged the stipends. Chasset said in his report that during their sittings a member had demanded that these stipends should not be provided by the State, but by the parishes: "No," said Chasset. "Public worship is a public service, it is the duty of us all; all are supposed to attend it. . . . The ministers of the altar constitute the spiritual militia which, like the army, gives help to all." Always there is this official presumption that all France is Catholic.

Stipends were approximately high for the superior clergy, and very fair for the inferior. Bishops received 12,000 to 20,000 francs; the vicars of cathedral churches from 2000 to 4000. Parish priests were divided into seven classes for the purpose of stipends, which ranged from 1200 to 4000 francs (6000 in Paris); curates (*vicaires*) got from 700 to 1200 francs.

This was a great boon to the lower clergy. No more poorly paid parish priests, no more inequalities, no more injustices, no more poverty. Instead, a comfortable income, a prospect of independence and prestige.

In all, the budget for public worship amounted to about 100,000,000.

Relations with the Pope were regulated by the following Article, which was inspired by that thoroughgoing Gallicanism which was lacking in the *Cahiers*: " A new bishop will not apply to the Pope for confirmation; but he will write to him as the visible head of the Universal Church to show the unity of the faith and the communion which he ought to maintain with him."

Such was the degree of independence of this Gallican Church as organized by the Constituent Assembly, and such was its constitution.

With no intention of schism, and not fearing it overmuch, the Assembly defined its design and its intentions, on 21st January 1791, in an instruction on the Civil Constitution, the whole of which must be quoted: " The representatives of the French, firmly attached to the religion of their fathers, to the Catholic Church whose visible head on earth is the Pope, have assigned the first place in the State budget to the expenses of public worship and its ministers; they have respected its doctrines, they have assured the continuance of its teaching. Convinced that Catholic faith and doctrine have their source in an authority more than human, they recognize that it is not for them to lay hands upon it, nor to attack an authority which is purely spiritual; they know that God Himself has established it, and has entrusted it to priests who are the shepherds of souls, that they may give them the help which religion offers to men, may hand on the apostolic succession, and enlighten and guide consciences." But the Assembly could legislate for the civil organization of the clergy and fix its external relations with the political order of the State: "It was impossible in a constitution based on equality, justice and the common good: equality which opens the public service to every man whose merits have been recognized by his fellow-citizens as rendering him worthy of it: justice which, to exclude all arbitrary acts, authorized only the deliberations in which all took part: the common good, which could not tolerate any parasitic establishment; it was impossible in such a constitution not to suppress many institutions which had become useless, not to establish the free election of priests, and not to require in all acts of ecclesiastical discipline that deliberations should be held in common, as this was the only guarantee in the eyes of the people of the wisdom of the decrees to which they would be called to submit."

These changes once made, the Ecclesiastical Committee of the Assembly watched zealously over the maintenance of those parts of the old Church discipline which they had not touched, and manifested a tendency to intervene directly in all the thorny questions of discipline. When, on 10th August 1791, the Abbé Bruyère, priest of St Paul's, Paris, asked if he might accede to the request of a priest who wanted Bruyère to marry him, Lanjuinais wrote a letter in the name of the Committee forbidding him to marry this priest. Thus, whether by the practice of the Civil Constitution or its fundamental principles —and especially by the State payment of the clergy—the bonds of Church and State were found to be drawn much more tightly than under the old régime, and the Church was more subordinated to the State.

That subordination became plainer and more rigorous when, on 27th November 1790, the Assembly formulated an oath to be taken by all priests expressive of adherence and loyalty to the Civil Constitution. As a matter of fact, it was this oath which was to break the union of Church and State by introducing discords which were the prelude to civil war.

§ VI

Birth of a religion of patriotism, federation, altars

Before discussing the practical results of the Civil Constitution, it is time to notice the growth of a new sentiment, that of revolutionary patriotism, which, at the very moment when the Assembly was discussing and passing the Civil Constitution, and rendering to the Catholic religion the homage we have just recorded, seemed to be taking a first place in the hearts of the French people as a sort of religion, better and more living than the old.

For ages past the French had loved their king and their country. But the leaders of French thought in the eighteenth century believed, as La Bruyère said in the time of Louis XIV., that under a despotism there is no country. There is no true country save where all are free, equal and brethren, where the people is self-governing and forms one family among the other families of nations. That is revolutionary patriotism.

This new patriotism, formulated more or less clearly by the philosophers, manifested itself in that great movement of revolt, liberation and union which was started in France by the taking of the Bastille. The emancipated communes united themselves into district federations, animated, one might say, by a centrifugal energy. These federations soon came to form only one—the national federation—which, on the Champ de Mars, at Paris, on 14th July 1790, took the oath to the new fatherland—regarded as one, free and equal; and the same day, in every commune of France, there was the same oath, the same ceremony.

The name of religion is the only one which can be applied to this movement of union. It was the religion of the fatherland. It had altars to the fatherland.

These altars were erected by the district federations in fairly large numbers. They were the centre of all the manifestations of the National Federation, not only in Paris and Lyons, but in all the towns and villages of which I have read the proceedings. Everywhere on this 14th July Frenchmen stood round the altar of the fatherland. These altars—of different forms in different places, but not modelled on the Catholic altar—were seldom or never set up in churches, but in the open air, in a public square, or a field. At this altar the civic oath was taken. Before this altar orators celebrated the praises of the fatherland.

Catholicism was represented at these ceremonies. If almost all the superior clergy turned away, the inferior clergy were present and took part. Generally, the two services, the old and the new, were performed separately before the same audience, who first went to Mass at church, and then betook themselves, often accompanied by the parish priests, to the altar of the fatherland. Sometimes, too, it happened that Mass was said on this very altar. It was so at Paris, where the Sacrament was celebrated in the Champ de Mars, on the national altar, by Bishop Talleyrand. Such a general participation of the clergy in the federations, often enthusiastic as it was, gave the impression that the Catholic religion had come to terms with the national religion—that is, with the Revolution—and that the French people could, for the moment, have the satisfaction of feeling themselves at once good patriots and good Catholics.

In reality, the competition of a new and strong religious sentiment brought no access of strength to the Catholic religion, although it afforded a proof of the popularity of the clergy. The Catholic religion was no longer the sole occupant of the realm of faith in the soul of the French people and, though perhaps it escaped their notice, its position of privilege and prestige was henceforth diminished. The patriotic revolutionary religion, vigorous and sturdy in the freshness of its youth, was not simply superimposed upon the old religion : it was mastering and even perhaps absorbing it.

This phenomenon, which passed unperceived, did not detach the people from the religion of their birth, but all unawares they came to regard it as less precious; and so the way was prepared from afar for that state of mind which rendered possible first an attempt to destroy Christianity and then the sway of the secular system.

One of the district federations—that of Strasbourg—had set an example of secularity, and this was the more remarkable because Alsace was the only part of France where liberty of worship existed under the old régime.

This example is important, not only as being unique, but because other departments, even as far off as Brittany, grouped themselves round the revolutionary altar of Strasbourg. At first, if Mass was said, the order ran that "only Catholics should be obliged to kneel," an expression of liberty which I have not found in any other federation. Liberty of conscience was then symbolized, on 16th June 1790, in the meadow where the Alsatians had set up their national altar, by three successive baptisms on the said altar. A Catholic infant had a Catholic for godfather and a Protestant for godmother, and a Protestant infant had a Protestant godfather and a Catholic godmother. Then, the priest and the pastor, who had each officiated in turn, embraced one another in the presence of the people.

In this wise the freedom of the two Christian cults was respected and practised in the "federation of the Rhine."

But the federation did not stop at a lesson of tolerance and charity. It proceeded to do homage to "philosophy." A third baptism followed—"a sort of civil baptism," as the report said. The "religious altar" was removed, and "the godmothers carrying the infants occupied its place." The flag of the federation was unfurled over their heads. The godfathers, in the name of the children, took the civic oath. The report stated that this sight "filled the soul with emotions impossible to describe." This ceremony almost foreshadowed the Worship of Reason and that of the Supreme Being, or at least the national religion organized as a *culte décadaire*.

As early then as June 1790, in a large gathering of

Frenchmen on the banks of the Rhine, the flag of liberty of conscience was boldly unfurled and the flag of philosophy as well.

These events, which synchronized with the drafting of the Civil Constitution, gave the lie to its principles and avowed aims. They were the first token of a new state of things, more in harmony with the real feelings of the philosophers, with the scepticism of a large part of the educated classes, and with the indifference or lukewarm faith of the ignorant, both artisans and peasants.

§ VII

The Pope pronounces against the Civil Constitution: the schism completed

Let us return to the Civil Constitution and its consequences.

After 10th July 1790, Pius VI. had written to Louis XVI. to beg him to refuse his sanction, threatening him with a "cruel religious war," and complaining also about the matters of Avignon. After much hesitation, on 24th August, Louis XVI. gave his sanction. But the Pope, who was always anxious and careful, did not hurry. A commission of cardinals examined the Civil Constitution at their leisure. The Pope was anxious to have the formal advice of the French episcopate. He soon had it, not from all the bishops, but from those who were members of the Constituent Assembly. On 30th October a manifesto was printed entitled: *Exposition of the Principles of the Civil Constitution of the clergy*. It was signed by Cardinal de La Rochefoucauld and by twenty-nine other episcopal deputies who had voted against the Civil Constitution.

Their argument was that the civil power cannot by itself alter the constitution of the Church: it needs the co-operation of the Church and therefore of the Pope.

These bishops, who afterwards refused to resign, admitted that the institution of bishops by metropolitans is in accordance with the ancient discipline of the Gallican Church. But for more than two centuries the Pope had instituted the bishops. "How could it have happened that he had not been consulted about the rights which the law allowed him?" As to the election of bishops, they regretted that the right to vote should be allowed to any elector provided he attended one Mass: "an oath and a profession of faith in the Catholic religion" ought to have been required. They rejected the election of parish priests: "There is not a single Catholic country in which the appointment of parish priests does not pertain in common law to the diocesan bishops." Moderate Gallicans as they were, they were careful, while defending the rights of the Pope, to define them, by recalling the definition given by Bossuet in his sermon on the unity of the Church. They denounced the Civil Constitution as schismatic. The civil power could not refuse the indispensable co-operation of the Church without arrogating to itself supremacy in purely spiritual matters, and over the spiritual jurisdiction of the Church; and that was the high road to schism, to a separation from the Universal Church, to another religion; to which it is impossible that the National Assembly should wish to lend its support and to submit the nation."

The thirty bishops protested beforehand against the civil power annulling the acts of jurisdiction of the bishops who wished to retain its exercise. Were they then going to leave all religions free " except that which was once supreme, which was maintained by the piety of our fathers and by all the laws of the State, and has been for twelve hundred years the national religion ?"

Finally they demanded the convocation of a National Council and also of Provincial Councils. They claimed " that recourse be had to the head of the Universal Church according to the ancient forms of the Gallican Church." They wished " to avoid schism." They wished " to employ every means which wisdom and charity could suggest to avert the troubles which might result in a deplorable schism."

On 10th March 1791 the Pope addressed an apostolic letter to Cardinal de La Rochefoucauld, the first signatory of the *Exposition of Principles*, in which brief he declared that he wished to have, before making any pronouncement, the general advice of the French bishops, and not only of thirty of them. It is quite possible that the notion of a National Council was displeasing to him, it always savoured of Gallicanism.

In his apostolical letter Pius VI. complained of the Civil Constitution, and criticized it, without for the present pronouncing a formal condemnation of it.

He had been sufficiently moderate not to continue to exact the payment of annates (thus accepting the decree of 4th August). This sacrifice had not been repaid : he had had "the sorrow of seeing several members of the National Assembly kindle, spread and keep up the fire of revolt at Avignon, against which we do not cease to protest and to invoke the rights of the Holy See."

As to the Civil Constitution, he declared it contrary both to doctrine and discipline, which was not surprising, since the National Assembly "neither thinks nor acts except to destroy religion and with it obedience to kings." He protested against the breach of the Concordat. He called the election of bishops "sacrilege." He argued that while Protestants were left in possession of their property, that of the clergy was confiscated. He said that State payment was dishonouring to the bishops, who were treated as hirelings, and that it was not enough. He protested against the abolition of the monastic orders. But in the end he did not condemn, he launched no anathema. He asked the French bishops to suggest a way of conciliation which should not be a contravention of doctrine or discipline. He said he wanted to do everything possible to avoid a schism.

The same day that the Pope communicated this Apostolical Brief to Louis XVI. he sent a covering letter, in which he lamented the deplorable state of the kingdom, *in quo basis ipsa religionis subvertitur, a nostro redemptore fundata*. On 13th April he addressed another Apostolical Brief to the bishops of France on the subject of the oath, in which he implored them, but in tones that were almost moderate, not to take the oath.

Pius VI. never received that general advice of the French episcopate for which he had asked. He reprimanded two bishops who took the oath—Talleyrand and Loménie de Brienne. He confined himself to this reprimand and to his two Apostolical Briefs. But these were regarded in

France, and everywhere else, as a formal condemnation of the Civil Constitution. The breach was complete: the papal nuncio was recalled—he left Paris on 31st May 1791. Louis XVI. had appointed M. de Ligue ambassador at Rome in place of Cardinal Bernis: the Pope refused to receive him. At the Palais Royal in Paris they burned the Pope in effigy. The seal, indeed, was set on the schism.

§ VIII

Division of the Gallican Church into jurors and non-jurors: quarrels

It cannot be said that this schism was a surprise to the National Assembly, which was almost resigned to it beforehand. What was a surprise to those who had believed that they were strengthening the unity of the Gallican Church was that this Church immediately split up, part remaining faithful to the Pope and rejecting the Civil Constitution, part accepting the Constitution and taking the oath.

What were the relative numbers? There are no complete statistics, except for the bishops, of whom it is known that only two took the oath. About the rest of the clergy there are only imperfect data. In the National Archives, in the papers of the Ecclesiastical Committee, there are the two lists of jurors and non-jurors drawn up by the directories of departments for forty-three departments. M. Sagnac has studied these statistics. He has found in these forty-three departments a total of 14,047 jurors against 10,395 non-jurors. There are great differences according to the district. In the Bas-Rhin there are 8 per cent. of jurors;

in the Haut-Rhin, 51 per cent.; in the Nord and the departments of Brittany, 20 per cent; in Dauphiné and Provence, 89 per cent.; in Var as much at 96 per cent. Information may be found in many monographs on the other departments. It seems probable that more than half of the clergy took the oath, perhaps three-fifths. But that was at first, during the first half of 1791. There were many retractions subsequently, after the Pope's briefs. How many? We do not know. It is possible that after these retractions the proportion of numbers would be changed in favour of the non-jurors, who were also called refractories, and against the jurors, also called Constitutionals, and that in the end the Gallican Church would be found divided into almost equal halves.

The result was disappointing to the Constituent Assembly, which had hoped to gather the whole Church into the new order of things; disappointing to the Pope, who in his brief of 10th March thought he was safe in saying that a very small number of priests had taken the oath—*perpauci secundi ordinis pastores infelicissimi.*

Public opinion—opinion in general, that of the "patriots," that of the militant revolutionaries—was incensed at this division, and there were violent popular demonstrations to re-establish by force the unity of the Gallican Church, which shows how far the masses still were from our idea of liberty of conscience.

The quarrel soon became very violent. The papal priests and their followers were treated as anti-revolutionists; the Constitutional priests and their followers were regarded as impious wretches, heretics, although the new clergy—the elected clergy—were equal to the refractory clergy in godliness and in morals. One may even say, without taking sides in this quarrel between believers, that the Constitutional episcopate surpassed in virtue and sincerity many bishops of the old régime.

The quarrel between refractories and Constitutionals became all at once so sharp that many directories of departments took measures which exceeded their competence. Thus the Directory of Finistère, together with the Constitutional Bishop Expilly, commanded refractory priests in April 1791 to withdraw within eight days to a distance of four leagues from their old parishes. Other directories, notably those of Ille-et-Vilaine and Ain, followed this example.

§ IX

Troubles in Paris and the first proclamation of liberty of worship

Some very lively incidents took place in Paris. Non-juring priests generally officiated in the chapels of nunneries. The people accused them of railing against the Revolution. There were serious acts of brutal intolerance. Some nuns were publicly whipped. They were accused, said the *Chronique de Paris*, of 9th April 1791, of having themselves "chastised some young girls who by their parents' orders had made their confession to a priest who was friendly to the new ecclesiastical laws." The papers added that "every day scenes of this sort are reported." The Directory of the Department of Paris, by a decree of 11th April 1791, denied non-juring priests the entry of these chapels, and also of the parish churches, but at the same time—and this caused a great sensation—it indirectly established liberty of worship by allowing sectaries of all kinds to hold services in their private houses if they refrained from all attack "upon the Constitution, the laws and established authorities," and if they placed above the principal entrance an inscription showing the use of the building.

The papal Catholics, with M. de Pancemont, ex-priest of Saint-Sulpice, a refractory, at their head, had hired the old church of the Théatins. They induced the Directory to agree to this inscription: "*Church consecrated to religious worship by a private Society. Peace and Liberty.*" On the opening day, 17th April, headed by the Abbé Latyl—a Constituent and Constitutional priest of Saint-Thomas—a violent hostile demonstration was made which was difficult to stop. The journals of the Left sided against this attempt to secure liberty of worship. One reads in the *Revolutions de Paris*: "The people have understood this objective better than their rulers: they feel that there cannot be two forms of worship in one religion."

Nevertheless a liberal movement was taking shape, even in governing circles, in the Constituent Assembly itself. The Abbé Siéyès—a member of the Assembly and also of the Directory of Paris—was one of the chiefs of this movement. The Constitutional Committee of the Assembly, to which this notorious resolution of the Directory was referred, appointed as its official reporter Talleyrand, who was in favour of liberty of worship, and even of what we call secularization. Noteworthy at this time was the decree of 4th April 1791, which on the occasion of the honours to be paid to the body of Mirabeau transformed the Church of Sainte-Geneviève into a civil

Pantheon in which were placed, by a decree of 30th May, the ashes of Voltaire. The very liberal resolution of the Directory of Paris, and the transformation of Sainte-Geneviève in honour of the most anti-Catholic writer of the century, were two notable incidents in the history of the once-dominant religion and of the peril in which it then stood.

Talleyrand's report marked a reaction against the views of the Constituent Assembly as to the unity of Catholic worship and the right of the State to enforce that unity. The liberty of conscience he demanded "is a real and complete liberty, a real property, not less inviolable than any other and claiming full protection." He added, disavowing indirectly the toleration established by the Declaration of Rights for opinions "even religious": "Let us not here speak of toleration; this overbearing word is an insult and ought to form no part of the speech of a free and enlightened people." A citizen may follow any religion he likes without thereby ceasing to be in any degree less a citizen. Talleyrand went so far as to say that the King, if he liked, might have a different religion from that of the nation. He called the Catholic religion true (*véritable*), but went on to say, and not without irony, that we should assure its triumph "by leaving to it nothing but the means of persuasion and showing that it has nothing to fear from rival sects." He rallied Treilhard and the Jansenist members of the Ecclesiastical Committee a little "who seemed to have seen in the Revolution only a splendid opportunity to deify the shades of Port Royal." In short, he proposed and got passed—though not without a lively debate and considerable opposition—a liberal decree which stated that the principles of religious liberty which inspired the decree of the Directory were the same that " the Assembly itself had recognized and embodied in its Declaration of Rights "—which was not true, as we know, but any appearance of amending the new gospel must be avoided. The Assembly went even further than the Directory : it declared that the fact of not having taken the oath cannot be brought up against any priest who presented himself in a parish church, chapel-of-ease or national oratory. But he must do nothing there except say Mass. It would of course have been impossible, in the state of passionate feelings then prevailing, to allow non-jurors to preach in parish churches.

It is evident that liberty of worship was rather wrenched from the men of the Revolution than granted by them of their free will. The Constituents recognized it in the decree of 7th May 1791, with a bad grace and many precautions and restrictions, but it was actually recognized, and it was a great step towards secularization.

§ X

Application of this liberty: non-jurors, Jews, Protestants

But popular opinion in Paris was not with the Assembly ; it would not listen to the only journalist whose voice was raised in favour of liberty and philosophy, I mean André Chénier.

When, on Ascension Day, 2nd June 1791, the papal Catholics—those may be so called who attended the ministrations of the non-juring priests—wished to resume the exercise of their worship in the church of the Théatins, they were prevented by a hostile crowd. La Fayette had to intervene with the National Guard. Bailly, the Mayor of Paris, reprehended violence in a public letter and preached liberty of worship, but in vain : the papal Catholics had to renounce their meetings in the church of the Théatins, which henceforth remained closed. They were obliged to refrain from the public exercise of their worship in Paris, and could assemble only privately, almost secretly, in the oratories and chapels of convents.

Did the other sects in Paris profit by the decree of 7th May 1791?

The position of the Jews does not seem to have been affected by it. The toleration which they had enjoyed for several years under the old régime was not suddenly changed into liberty. No doubt, on hearing that they were being persecuted in Lorraine and Alsace, the Constituent Assembly directed its president, on 28th September 1789, to write and tell the municipal authorities of those districts that the Declaration of Rights applied to Jews, and that they also were under the protection of the law. But it was only a nominal protest. On 24th December the Assembly refused to come to any decision as to their civil status. On 28th January 1790 it recognized that Portuguese, Spanish and Avignon Jews were to be allowed to exercise the rights of citizens, but citizenship was not granted to other Jews. It was not until the very last days of its existence, on 27th September 1791, that the Assembly revoked " all adjournments, reservations and exceptions in the foregoing decrees with regard to individual Jews who shall be willing to take the civic oath, which will be regarded as a renunciation of all privileges and exceptions previously made in their favour."

As to their worship, since 1787 the Jews had had several synagogues in Paris. These sufficed them under the Revolution. After the decree of 7th May 1791 it was rumoured that they were going to buy or hire the churches. They did nothing of the kind. Prudently, and half in hiding, they contented themselves with the practical toleration they already enjoyed.

And the Protestants? Since the revocation of the Edict of Nantes and the demolition of the temple of Charenton the Lutherans of Paris had held their meetings in the Chapel of the Swedish Embassy, and the Calvinists in the Chapel of the Dutch Embassy. The edict of 1787 encouraged them to reconstitute their Church. They took for their pastor Marron, the chaplain of the Dutch Embassy, and grandson of a French refugee. They asked authorization to hold their meetings together. The Government hesitated, held an inquiry, and ended by refusing, saying that the embassy chapels should suffice.

The Lutherans, under the Revolution, seem to have gone on contentedly using the Chapel of the Swedish Embassy, as under the old régime.

But the Calvinists, who were much more numerous, appear to have been granted from the outset of the Revolution a sort of verbal authorization for the exercise of their worship. They had in consequence hired a room in a restaurant in the Rue Mondétour, which they had used as a place of worship since 7th June 1789. After the passing of Article 13 of the Declaration, which enlarged the bounds of toleration, they set about obtaining a more suitable place of worship. One of them, Rabaut Saint-Étienne, dissuaded them, saying that the time was not ripe. Therefore, to avoid all demonstration and not to run counter to public opinion, they remained in their humble abode in the Rue Mondétour until February 1790. M. Armand Lods, their historian, tells us that they then hired the former Hall of the Sons of Apollo, called the "Museum," in the Rue Dauphine. The decree of 7th May 1791 gave them further courage. They hired the Church of Saint-Louis-du-Louvre, turned it into their place of worship, and on 22nd May it was solemnly dedicated. Pastor Marron had the following inscription placed over the front, with the approval of the Directory of the department: "*This Year of Christ* 1791 *and Year II. of Liberty. A building consecrated to religious worship by a private Society. Peace and Liberty.*" Inside, the symbols of the Catholic religion were replaced by two marble tablets on which were engraved the Declaration of Rights and the Lord's Prayer.

The Protestants gathered there in public without meeting with any opposition from the people of Paris, who were so intolerant towards the papal Catholics. They had the support, the favour, and sometimes even the presence of the authorities. When the King had accepted the Constitution they celebrated, on 13th October 1791, a thanksgiving service in the presence of the municipality, whom they had invited, and who were represented by twelve municipal officers and by the mayor, Bailly. "There was a great crowd," said a contemporary report; "there were many Calvinists and more philosophers, anxious to enjoy the firstfruits of toleration." Pastor Marron praised the Revolution: "What distinguishes it," he said, "is that it is entirely the work of reason. . . . It has not given us a change of masters: it has given us more freedom." The listeners were so pleased and touched by these words that they wept.

§ XI

Non-jurors appear as anti-revolutionists

This tolerance and sympathy for Protestants showed up in strong contrast the unpopularity of the non-juring clergy.

The non-juring bishops were forced either to emigrate or go into hiding, but they continued to direct their dioceses in secret, either in person or through their rural deans. The bishops—who were nearly all of the upper classes—looked back with regret to their privileges and to the old régime. The non-juring parish priests were thus drawn into aristocratic circles. It must be admitted that these non-juring priests gave proof of their disinterestedness. They vowed themselves to poverty by renouncing beforehand the State pay, which was withdrawn by the decree of 29th November 1791, and, moreover, the Church had lost its property. They were enthusiasts, ready to make any sacrifice for their cause, even to endure martyrdom, and it was for that reason they were so dangerous.

Persecution fanned their zeal.

The law of 27th November 1790, on the oath, enjoined the prosecution "as disturbers of public order" of non-juring priests "who took part in any public functions or in those which they exercised as a body." The law of 7th May 1791 explicitly allowed them to say Mass—but nothing save Mass—in parish churches, and implicitly allowed them to exercise their full functions in buildings other than parochial. But what was to be understood by "public functions"? The Constituent Assembly always refused to give a clear definition. On 19th June 1791 Treilhard got a law passed that public prosecutors should be *bound*, under penalty of forfeiture and dismissal, to prosecute all non-juring priests who continued to exercise "the same public functions." In practice there was at first a tendency to consider as usurping public functions only such priests as did not limit themselves to saying Mass but in addition heard confessions and performed the rites of baptism, marriage and funerals. Public opinion would not allow them to come into competition with the Constitutional clergy.

Was this competition serious? What following had the refractory clergy in point of numbers and importance? It is impossible to give figures. The numbers of the faithful who rallied round the non-juring clergy evidently varied in different places. There were more in Brittany, La Vendée and Lozère than in the departments of the Île-de-France. There were more where the priest was beloved, and especially in the countryside where, when the old religion was preferred, it was due to habit or friendship. Everything leads us to think that the sectaries of the papal persuasion were much fewer in proportion to the number of the population than the non-juring priests to the total number of clergy.

The non-juring clergy, who were granted some measure

of liberty by the decree of 7th May, were much hampered by the question of localities, in the country districts if not in towns. The suppression of parishes and convents in most towns made churches and chapels available which they could buy or hire. In the rural parts, where there was only one church to a commune, it was the parish church, the church of the Constitutional vicar, and it was not easy to find another building. If the rich man or the former squire opened the chapel of his château to the non-jurors, such congregations were dispersed as anti-revolutionary. In those country places where the peasantry were most pious, or most devoted to their old priests, they exercised their worship in woods or open fields. No doubt this did not often happen, and there is no need to conclude from these exceptional cases that the persecution was general, nor that the revival of religious fervour was widespread, nor that a sort of primitive Christianity was reborn in rural districts. What is certain is that Catholics everywhere were divided into two hostile parties, who hated each other more day by day, quarrelled more, and sometimes came to blows.

The attitude of local authorities differed widely. It appears that the departmental directories, following the lead of the Directory of Paris, were for giving liberty to the non-jurors, and that the municipalities, following the lead of the municipality of Paris, were against it. Thus, at Pamiers the papal Catholics hired the church which had belonged to the Carmelites and the Department of Ariège sanctioned this inscription for it: "*Love of God and one's neighbour. Respect and obedience to the law. Peace and Charity.*" But the "patriots" of Pamiers opposed this public exercise of papal worship. There were disturbances. The municipality closed the church. The Directory of the department ordered it to be reopened. The municipality refused. In vain the Directory insisted and issued new decrees; the municipality had the last word. In the Tarn the Directory of the department could not prevent the municipality of Lisle, instigated and favoured by the Constitutional vicar, and in opposition to the non-juring priest who was not allowed to say his Mass in the parish church except with closed doors, from issuing a decree according to which "any sick person who has not called in the vicar (Constitutional) within five days of the beginning of his illness shall be considered to have renounced the Catholic religion and shall be deprived, if he dies, of Christian burial; the vicar shall go, accompanied by such persons as he chooses, to the houses of the sick, and those who refuse his spiritual aid shall be prosecuted during life and after death, the vicar having the power to dig up the corpse." The National Guard lent its aid to the execution of these tyrannical measures.

But many tolerant municipalities also existed—Autun, for instance—and on the other hand some directories were hostile to liberty of worship, such as the departments of Brittany. In the district of Chatillon (Deux-Sèvres) and in the Department of La Vendée, quarrels were so violent that, by order of the National Assembly, the Minister of Justice sent down two commissioners, Gallois and Gensonné, to make an inquiry and restore order. Their report shows the devotion of the peasants of La Vendée to the non-juring priests, and how, for love of them, their attachment to the Revolution had cooled. The commissioners decided to suspend the application of the decree of 7th May 1791 in this district and to reject the petitions of the non-jurors for the hire of churches for their worship. "As these petitions," they said, "which we know are instigated most warmly by the persons who do not sign them, appear to us to form part of a larger and more secret scheme, we have not thought proper to legislate for a religious separation which we believe, given the time and the situation of the department, to harbour all the germs of a civil breach among the citizens."

This did not prevent the Assembly, on 9th August 1791, from inserting in the Constitution an Article guaranteeing "liberty to every man to practise the worship to which he is attached." The police regulation of 19th July 1791 had imposed fine and imprisonment on "those who shall insult the objects of any worship whatever, whether in a public book, or in places devoted to the exercise of that worship, or ministers in the exercise of their functions, or who shall interrupt with public disturbance the services of any religion whatever."

§ XII

Severe laws against them; measures of secularization

Habit and passion were stronger than the laws. Under the Legislative Assembly liberty was more and more refused to Nonconformists. The refractory clergy, directed by bishops who had almost all emigrated, were hated by the "patriots," who feared them as anti-revolutionaries, and, in fact, that was what they became more and more. The "patriots" had got the idea that the Revolution must either crush the refractory clergy or be crushed by them. Under the pressure of this feeling, which was general in the clubs, sections and newspapers of the Left, the Legislative Assembly, after a long debate, passed a political-religious decree (29th November 1791). They abolished the obligation to take the special oath which had served as pretext for the schism of the refractories. Nothing was to be required from priests but the civic oath imposed on all officials; in this way they would see, so they said, who were the priests eager to conspire against the country. If a priest refused the civic oath, the Directory of his department might banish him provisionally from his ordinary place of residence; and priests who incited to disobedience to the laws or the authorities were to be punished by detention for two years. The decree of 7th May 1791 was thus revoked in two of its provisions: henceforth the parish churches were to be used exclusively for the official worship, and no priest was to be allowed to minister in the other churches unless he had taken the civic oath. The King refused his sanction. But in forty-two departments the authorities enforced the decree as if it had become law. Thus from December 1791, throughout the greater part of France, there was no liberty of religious worship for papal Catholics, although the Government persisted in demanding the application of the laws.

The spirit of the Legislative Assembly was no longer that of the authors of the Civil Constitution, and the citizens who had elected the Assembly had to witness the rebuff administered to the Constitution. The Assembly could not have succeeded without the general adhesion of the clergy and the faithful; it had aimed at the unity of the Gallican Church under the authority of the State, and had caused a split which arrayed about half the clergy against the State. That state of things brought into light the idea of secularization—of separation. The idea had the support of the Press, even of the Left. On 16th May 1792 the Abbé de Moy, an ex-noble, deputy for Paris, and Constitutional vicar of Saint-Laurent, made a strong speech from the rostrum of the Legislative Assembly, demanding the abolition of the Civil Constitution and of the subvention to the expenses of public worship; he also demanded religious liberty—except that priests should be banished from the kingdom who preached or professed maxims contrary to the Constitution—without, however, binding any priest to take the civic oath.

This motion, which would have been displeasing to the Constituent Assembly, was applauded sympathetically by the Legislative Assembly. But it thought that the time was not ripe to make experiments in liberty, seeing that France had been in a state of war since 20th April 1792, when her territory had been threatened by invasion on the part of the Prussians, the Austrians and the *émigrés*, whose accomplices at home seemed to be the refractory clergy. It was, then, by way of national defence, and apparently for the safety of the country, that on 27th May 1792 the Assembly passed a severer decree against the non-juring clergy than that of 29th November: "seeing that the constant attempts of the non-juring clergy to overthrow the Constitution forbid us to think that they wish to join in the social pact, and seeing that the public safety would be endangered by regarding as members of society persons who are only anxious to destroy it, and considering that the laws are powerless against these men," the Legislative Assembly established measures of administration against them. Any non-juring priest might be banished if twenty citizens, having the right to vote and belonging to the same canton, demanded it, and the measure should be taken by the department on the advice of the district.

If the department and the district could not agree, an inquiry was to be held, and sentence given. If one or more citizens gave information of disturbances excited by overt acts of a non-juror, the department, having verified the charge, should pronounce his banishment to such country as the non-juror should choose. If a non-juror persisted in staying in France, or should return to it, he should be liable to ten years' imprisonment.

The King refused his sanction, and this was one of the great grievances against him. This decree, like that of 29th November 1791, was enforced as law by several directories of departments (*e.g.* that of Charente). On 10th August 1792, when the insurrection was victorious, the Legislative Assembly decided that the decrees which had not received the Royal sanction should have the force of law, and thus those of 29th November and 27th May became law. They were rendered more severe, under the pressure of external danger and the feelings inspired by the approach of the Austrians and Prussians, by the decree of 26th August, which compelled all non-juring priests—except infirm persons and those over sixty—to leave France within a fortnight, or be deported to Guiana. The oath of liberty and equality, in force since 15th August

1792, was exacted of all priests. As very few Nonconformists took it, it may be said that when the Legislative Assembly broke up there was no more liberty for papal Catholics. Denounced, hunted, imprisoned, deported, sometimes put to death (by subsequent laws), though in the eyes of the faithful they appeared as martyrs, the fact that they could be chased, brutally treated, outraged with impunity as public enemies, reacted injuriously on the Catholic religion itself—which was more endeared to the rural masses by its ministers than by its doctrines. The sight of priests scouted and persecuted paved the way for the sight of religion scouted and persecuted.

While the Legislative Assembly was passing cruel measures against refractory priests the idea of the secular State was gaining ground—as witness the affair of the Corpus Christi Day processions in Paris, in June 1792. Up till then the inhabitants had been accustomed to drape and decorate the walls of their houses on this occasion. In 1790 and 1791 the municipality had renewed the old police regulations on that head. On 20th June 1792, on the demand of Manuel, procurator of the commune, it enjoined that no citizen be obliged to do this, and that this expenditure should be "purely voluntary"; that nothing must be done to infringe the liberty of religious opinion; that the National Guard must not be employed in any religious ceremony; that shopkeepers were in no way obliged to shut their shops. This seemed very bold. Camille Desmoulins wrote: "Kings are ripe but God not yet." Brissot on the other hand lent the measure his fervent support in *The French Patriot.* The Directory of the Department of Paris gave its approval. What was still more significant was that the Legislative Assembly, which had been invited by the vicar of Saint-Germain-l'Auxerrois to take part in the procession, first accepted and then revoked its decree, deciding that it would not sit on that day, so that its members in their private capacity might take part in the procession. It behaved almost as if there were no longer a State religion—as if the State were purely secular.

That did not prevent it from shielding the Revolution against ecclesiastical persons other than refractory priests —I mean congregations of regulars and even of seculars. The Constituent Assembly, as we have seen, had suppressed all orders and congregations under vows. But nuns were allowed to remain in their convents, and monks who refused to leave had been collected in different houses. Many monks sided against the Revolution and meddled in the intrigues of the refractory priests. The Legislative Assembly decreed, on 4th August 1792, that all houses then occupied by monks or nuns should be evacuated and put up for sale. The only exception was in favour of nuns nursing in hospitals and in other charitable institutions.

The Constituent Assembly had refused to take any measure against the secular congregations. Some of them, such as the priests of the Oratory, were liked and respected. But here, also, many individuals had taken sides against the Revolution. On 18th August 1792 the Legislative Assembly suppressed all congregations without exception, even Sisters of Charity. Ex-nuns might be employed in hospitals in a private capacity, and those who were engaged in education might continue their work.

Congregations, whether regular or secular, had henceforth no existence of any kind, and the Catholic Church thus suffered loss in France by the disappearance of an important and militant part of its clergy.

An event still more serious, perhaps, was the secularization of the parish registers, decreed by the Legislative Assembly in its last session on 20th September 1792. This secularization had been demanded by the papal Catholics. Placed by circumstances in a situation analogous to that of the Protestants after the edict of 1787, they were not allowed, as were the latter, to do without the parish priest and apply to the local magistrate in matters touching their civil status: they were obliged to apply to the Constitutional priest, and that they would not do; they therefore asked that the registers of civil status should be put into the hands of civil officials. The Constituent Assembly at first turned a deaf ear. On 27th August 1791 it decreed that the method of notification of births, deaths and marriages should be arranged by the future National Assembly. But at the same time it indicated the spirit in which this arrangement should be made, when it declared that "the law considers marriage as a civil contract and nothing more." The Legislative Assembly then entrusted the registration of births, marriages and deaths to municipal officers, thus establishing the system which still exists to-day. At the same time—and this was a serious blow to religion—it established and organized the possibility of divorce by an inference from that Article of the Constitution which states that "the law considers marriage as simply a civil contract." Thus, when the National Convention met, and the Republic replaced the Monarchy, the Catholic religion, alike in its moral authority and its prestige, had recently suffered several reverses.

CHAPTER III

CHAPTER III

THE ATTEMPT TO DESTROY CHRISTIANITY, 1793-1794

§ I

The Convention at first maintains the Civil Constitution

ELECTED as it was by universal suffrage, when the people were for the most part illiterate, it would have been natural for the National Convention to be less philosophic than the Legislative Assembly which had been chosen by duly qualified and enlightened electors. However, the citizens who had previously been disqualified, but were now enfranchised, made little use of their right to vote. The influence of the peasants was hardly felt in the new Assembly. Nevertheless, it included several members of the Constituent Assembly and some members of the Ecclesiastical Committee which had drawn up the Civil Constitution—such as Camus and Treilhard. Thus at first the Convention seemed resolved to maintain that Constitution.

On 13th November 1792, Cambon announced to the Convention that the Finance Committee, of which he was reporter, was preparing a Bill for the abolition of the budget of public worship, but the Convention would not sanction it. On the contrary it decreed, on 30th November, on the motion of Danton, "that they had never intended to deprive the citizens of the ministrations of religion, which the Civil Constitution of the clergy had given them." They repeated the same declaration on 11th January 1793; and on 27th June following, although some Constitutional bishops had abetted the federal insurrection, the Convention decreed that the payment of ecclesiastics forms part of the public debt.

On 23rd March 1793, bishops, incumbents and curates were legally exempted from liability to military service. (A decree of 10th December previous had confirmed their status as public officials.) On 27th March, Carra and Auguis, representatives *en mission*, told the Vendeans, in the name of the Convention, that the Republic was founded on the teaching of the Gospel. Corpus Christi Day processions took place in Paris on 30th May 1793, freely and without disturbances. The Constitution of 1793 proclaimed liberty of conscience.

During the first months of its existence the Convention seized every opportunity to affirm and proclaim, not merely that it did not mean to destroy religion, but that it intended to maintain the Gallican system of Church incorporate in the State—that is, the Civil Constitution of the clergy.

§ II

Hostile attitude of the Pope; La Vendée; severe laws against refractory priests

At the same time the Convention was enforcing and even increasing in severity the laws against refractory or non-juring priests—that is, the papalists. Their papalism seemed really intolerable now that the Pope was siding with the enemies of France. A serious incident occurred. Bassville, a French diplomat, secretary of legation at Naples, had been sent to Rome to protect the interests of French merchants there. He hoisted the tricolour flag over his house. His servants wore the tricolour cockade. The Roman mob killed him (13th January 1793). The murderers went unpunished, and this led to the belief that the Papal Government was concerned in the murder. An explosion of wrath took place at Paris against the Pope, who was regarded as the soul of the coalition against France. The non-juring clergy, who had been so devoted to this hostile Pope, were still further discredited, and a part of this discredit perhaps fell upon the Constitutional Church, which, though it had separated itself from the Pope on certain points of discipline, venerated him as "the visible head of the Universal Church," and loudly disavowed any idea of schism. In France the murder of Bassville was an injury to the Catholic religion itself. It was one of those events which rendered possible an attempt to destroy Christianity.

But what most harmed religion at that moment was the part manifestly taken by non-juring priests in the insurrection of La Vendée. No doubt the raising of 300,000 men was the immediate occasion of the insurrection, on account of the reluctance which the Vendeans felt to engaging in military service far from home. But these armed rebels called themselves "Royal and Catholic armies." The priests fanned the flame, while the royalists turned the insurrection to their own profit. The civil war in La Vendée, by which Republican France was stabbed in the back at the very moment when she was struggling with foreign foes, was the danger-point of the Revolution —a danger which might have been fatal—and of this the people, in Paris and the towns especially, were well aware. It was a crime against the fatherland, that young

fatherland so religiously adored—a crime which seemed horrible and inexpiable. The priests were thought to be the accomplices or even the instigators of the crime. The non-juring clergy were the enemy, and if the religion which had such ministers was not yet identified with the foe, it nevertheless incurred suspicion through the attitude of these unpatriotic priests.

Of all the events that wrought the frame of mind which resulted in the attempt to dethrone Christianity, the insurrection of La Vendée, by its clerical form, was the chief, the most influential. I might almost say that without La Vendée there would have been no Worship of Reason. The immediate result of the insurrection was an increased severity in the laws against non-juring priests.

On 13th March 1793 the Convention passed the death penalty on priests compromised in the disturbances excited by the recruiting. The same day it decreed that such priests as were under sentence of transportation, and caught within the territory of the Republic, should be brought before a military jury, and put to death within twenty-four hours. On 23rd April it decreed that priests who had not yet taken the oath to maintain liberty and equality should be immediately transported to Guiana. The 29th and 30th Vendémiaire of the Year II. witnessed a terrible law. Priests holding communication with the enemies of the fatherland, whether at home or abroad, were to be put to death within twenty-four hours after having been found guilty, by a military commission, of bearing arms; and "the fact shall be considered as proved either by a written declaration with two signatures, or by one signature attested by one witness, or by the oral statement of two witnesses, provided that they agreed." As for such priests as had returned to France, they might be put to death if two witnesses agreed that they were under sentence of transportation. The most novel feature of the law, and a great aggravation of its severity, was that it struck also at the Constitutional clergy. It enjoined the transportation of all ecclesiastics who, though they had taken the oaths, should be denounced for want of patriotism (*incivisme*) by six citizens of their canton, after this denunciation had been "adjudicated on by the Directory of the department on the advice of the district."

This law thus placed all the Catholic clergy under legal suspicion, jurors as well as non-jurors, official priests as well as those who were no longer in the exercise of their functions. The Convention, then, had changed its attitude towards the Constitutional Church. Why? In the first place, because the Constitutional Church had not served the purpose for which it was created, for it had not the unity of a National Church, and it was doing nothing to achieve this unity. It was not, therefore, strong enough for the Republic to lean upon. Again, since 2nd June 1793—the date of the appearance of the revolutionary faction known as the Mountain—it became plain that the Mountain could not count on the Constitutional Church, many of whose ministers had made common cause with the Girondists and federalists, and were plunged in a plot for civil war as dangerous as that of La Vendée. So the Constitutional clergy were also the enemy in the eyes of a Montanist and "Sansculotte" populace. It seemed to them that these priests were not a whit better than the others; that Girondist jurors were just as dangerous as the non-jurors—the accomplices of kings and *émigrés*. Was it not true that the Constitutionals had taken part with the federalists, just as the refractories had done in the insurrection of La Vendée? People thought so and said so, perhaps on insufficient grounds. But it is certain that Constitutional bishops had marched against the Mountain together with the administrative authorities of the revolted departments; and in Paris especially, and other towns, this grievance grew in the popular imagination. They extended their suspicions, though less noisily, to the Protestant clergy, whose most eminent and famous member, Rabaut Saint-Étienne, a member of the National Convention, had openly taken part against the Mountain. Marron, the pastor of the Calvinistic Church in Paris, was arrested as a moderate on 21st September 1793 and kept in prison for several days.

§ III

First movements and measures of dechristianization

Till now the people had distinguished between good priests and bad. Now they began to think that there were no more good priests. The Catholic religion was discredited in the eyes of many militant patriots. They said that if religion was a hindrance to national defence, an obstacle in the way of Revolution, then religion must be abolished. The idea was spread by the anxiety of exasperated patriotism. The unbelief of certain followers of the philosophers, certain journalists, clubmen and municipal officers of Paris, blew these first sparks of destructive free-thought into a conflagration.

Moreover, the sanctuary could now be violated with less difficulty than of old ; it had lost its prestige ever since the people had entered it to enforce the decrees of the Constituent and Legislative Assemblies (29th September 1789, 10th to 12th September 1792) which sent to the Mint all church plate except the indispensable minimum, and also to enforce the decree of the Convention (23rd July 1793) which ordered the melting down for cannon of all church bells, leaving only one to each parish.

Sacrilege, almost official in character, had been committed—as at Rheims, on 7th October 1793, when Ruhl, a member of the Convention, broke the Holy Ampulla with his own hands.

The marriage of priests was a matter of jest to those who were not scandalized, and the prestige of religion suffered thereby. One of the first instances was that of Thomas Lindet, Bishop of the Eure, who took a wife in November 1792. Pontard, Bishop of the Dordogne, introduced his wife to the Convention at its session of 22nd September 1793. President Cambon gave a fraternal ceremonial embrace to these couples. The time was past when the Ecclesiastical Committee of the Constituent Assembly could forbid priests to marry. The Convention favoured priests who were legally married. It enjoined that, if their parishioners turned them out, they should keep their pay (19th July 1793); that all dismissals of married priests be reversed (12th August); that the stipends of priests who had been molested because of their marriage should be chargeable to the communes

which persecuted them, and that these priests might take their pay and spend it where they liked (15th November 1793). In fact, the Convention set up a condition of privilege for married priests. They numbered more than two thousand, says their historian, the Constitutional Bishop Grégoire, who himself was unmarried.

The movement for the destruction of Christianity began in the provinces, under the auspices of certain representatives *en mission*, who had no sort of authority for their doings. Thus Fouché, at Nevers, in a proclamation of 26th September 1793, falsely claimed to be authorized by the Convention "to substitute the religion of the Republic and natural morality for the superstitious and hypocritical cults to which the people are still so unfortunately devoted." On 10th October he passed a decree upon cemeteries; not content with proscribing all their religious emblems, he ordered an inscription above the gate: "*Death is eternal sleep.*" On 16th October Chaumette, who met Fouché at Nevers, got the Commune of Paris to approve of this decree, at least in principle. At Rochefort, Laignelot turned the parish church into a "Temple of Truth," which, on 31st October, witnessed a grand ceremony—namely, the abdication of eight Catholic priests and of one Protestant minister.

On the other hand, the Commune of Paris, on the motion of Chaumette, 23rd Vendémiaire of the Year II., decreed that no minister of any religion whatever should appear out of doors in any but civilian attire.

The Convention itself had for some time past assumed a "philosophic" attitude which furnished the occasion or the incentive to audacious acts. The festival of 10th

August 1793 was the first of the national fêtes which had a purely civic or, as we should say, secular character. Hérault de Séchelles, a member of the Convention, who presided, seemed to deify Nature, whose statue was honoured by libations. On 2nd October following, the Convention decreed that the ashes of Descartes be transferred to the Panthéon, on a report by Marie-Joseph Chénier, which read: "If Descartes had done nothing but substitute new errors for old ones, he would still have rendered a great public service by leading men to examine and not to believe."

The establishment of the republican era—that is, the substitution of the republican calendar for the Gregorian (decrees of 5th October 1793 and 4th Frimaire of the Year II.)—was a political move, but it was also anti-religious, as appears from the reports of Fabre d'Églantine and of Romme, which are full of philosophic attacks upon dogma. To substitute other dates and other festivals for the usual ones, to abolish Sunday and substitute the tenth day, to replace the names of the saints by those "of objects which constitute true national wealth," was to tear from Catholicism a part of its adornments and prestige, nay, to drive it violently out of the ordinary life of the nation. This decree horrified foreigners: they thought that France had already destroyed Christianity within its borders.

The Committee of Public Instruction of the Convention had become a home of propaganda against Catholicism. Grégoire states that Fourcroy said to him, repeating the phrase of Voltaire: "This infamous religion must be crushed." On 26th June 1793 Lakanal had proposed, in the name of the Committee, a series of national festivals, which in due course took the place of religious festivals. This committee struck a direct blow at the Catholic Church by its decree of 7th Brumaire of the Year II., which declared that for the future no ecclesiastic or nun could be appointed teacher in a school. On the 15th Brumaire of the Year II. the Convention applauded, and had printed, a speech in which Marie-Joseph Chénier, in the name of the Committee, proposed to substitute the religion of the fatherland for Catholicism : "Wrench," he said, "the sons of the Republic from the yoke of theocracy which now weighs upon them . . . then, freed from prejudice and worthy to represent the French nation, you will be able, on the ruins of fallen superstitions, to found the one universal religion, which has neither secrets nor mysteries, whose one dogma is equality, whose orators are the laws, whose pontiffs are the magistrates, which asks no incense from the great human family to burn save before the altar of our country, our mother, and our deity."

§ IV

Initiative of the citizens of Ris-Orangis, who renounced their religion ; abdications ; Festival of Reason at Notre-Dame

It was Ris-Orangis, a little rural commune in the middle of the Île-de-France, which set the first example of throwing Christianity overboard. The patron saint of the parish was Saint Blaise. A young volunteer having spoken of Brutus to the inhabitants, they took down Saint Blaise, put Brutus up in his place—even gave his name to their commune—and dismissed their vicar. The neighbouring communes did the same, and on the 10th Brumaire of the Year II. the administrators of the district of Corbeil came and declared to the Convention that most of their fellow-citizens had no religion now " but that of liberty." The Convention gave them honourable mention and a paragraph in the *Bulletin*. On the 16th Brumaire the people of Mennecy (in this same district of Corbeil) appeared at the bar of the Chamber wearing copes, in derision, and declared that they had no more need of a parish priest; that they had abjured superstition; had put up the busts of Le Peletier and Marat in their houses instead of those of Saints Peter and Paul, and had set up a statue of Liberty on the High Altar of what had been their parish church. Before rising, and on the motion of Barère, reporter of the Committee of Public Safety, the Convention recognized " the right of all citizens to adopt whatever religion they like and to suppress the ceremonies they do not like," and it gave to the directories of departments the power to decide finally on the suppression of parish churches. But the Convention, in spite of the philosophic attitude it had taken up, followed rather than favoured the movement.

This movement went so far at Paris that Gobel, the Constitutional Bishop of Paris, on the injunction of certain militant free-thinkers, such as Anacharsis Cloots, a member of the Convention, decided to renounce his functions, with eleven of his priests (without, however, apostatizing). He appeared at the bar of the Convention on the 17th Brumaire of the Year II., announced his resignation, put off his cross and ring, and put on the red cap. The ecclesiastical members of the Convention did the same at this and the following sittings, with some few exceptions, of whom Grégoire was one. The Protestant pastors who were members of the Convention also resigned—like Julien de Toulouse and Lombard-Lachaux. Pastor Marron at Paris did the same, or nearly the same. On the 20th Brumaire of the Year II. he brought to the Commune the four silver cups which had been used as chalices at the Church of Saint-Louis-du-Louvre, and, without formally saying that he renounced his functions, he condemned theology and paid homage to the "eternal and immortal principles of fact and morality." Scenes of patriotic enthusiasm followed.

As a result of these striking examples there were numerous resignations of vicars and curates throughout the whole of France.

On the very evening of this 17th Brumaire the Commune and the Department of Paris decreed that the next tenth-day festival, 20th Brumaire, should be kept at Notre-Dame, that a statue of Liberty should be set up "instead and in place of the former image of the Blessed Virgin," and Pache, Mayor of Paris, styled this ceremony the "Festival of Liberty and Reason."

The ceremony of the 20th Brumaire was very important. The insignia of the Catholic religion in the Church of Notre-Dame had been covered up, and a mound had been heaped up, on which stood a Greek temple, with an inscription—"To Philosophy"—and with four busts of philosophers, no doubt those of Voltaire, Rousseau, Franklin and, perhaps, Montesquieu. The "Torch of Truth" flamed upon an altar. Young girls defiled in procession; they were clad in white, with tricolour sashes, wore wreaths of flowers and carried torches. Then there emerged from the temple a beautiful woman, dressed in a mantle of blue and wearing the red cap. As the personification of Liberty she received the homage of the Republicans, who, stretching their hands toward her, sang a hymn by Marie-Joseph Chénier:

> "Come, holy Liberty, inhabit this temple,
> Become the goddess of the French people."

The whole scene was enacted artistically and tastefully by actresses from the Opera.

Then the Department and the Commune assembled at the bar of the Convention, where Chaumette declared, in their name, that the people wanted no other priests or gods than those which nature offers us: "We, their magistrates, have gathered from their lips this expression of their wish, and we bring it to you from the Temple of Reason"; and he asked that henceforth Notre-Dame should be known as the Temple of Reason. A decree to this effect was immediately passed. The actress who had represented Liberty took her place in the office, where the President and secretaries gave her the ceremonial embrace of welcome. Then the Convention repaired to Notre-Dame, where the ceremony was repeated in its honour.

The next day, the 21st, the Convention received a deputation from the popular clubs of Paris asking it to suppress the stipends of priests. The request was honourably mentioned, but adjourned.

§ V

Nature and diffusion of the Worship of Reason

The movement of dechristianization quickly became general in Paris. Almost all parts of the town renounced religion, closed the parish churches, and then reopened them as Temples of Reason.

On the 23rd Brumaire the Protestants of Paris followed suit: they brought to the Commune the few silver cups which their worship required. The President replied that if any religion were to be preserved it was the Protestant; but, he said, we must have no other religion than that of Liberty and Equality.

The chapels of the Calvinists seem after that to have been deserted, at least in Paris. For in Prairial of the Year II. Pastor Marron was denounced and arrested, for the second time, for having solemnized a marriage in his chapel, which shows that the people believed that no worship ought to have been held there. He remained in prison till the fall of Robespierre, and during his captivity Protestant worship was not celebrated, either at Saint-Louis or (it would seem) anywhere else. Nevertheless, by the end of October 1793, the Calvinists at Paris had given a signal token of good will by transferring their Sunday service to the tenth day.

The Lutherans, who were less numerous and less well known, were able to continue their worship in the Chapel of the Swedish Embassy. The chaplain, Gambs, took the precaution to transfer the services from Sunday to the tenth day, and this plan was more successful with him than with the Calvinists. As to the Lutherans in Alsace, we know that their places of worship were closed, like all other churches.

The Convention had not abolished the Catholic religion, but it was well on the way to it. On the 25th Brumaire it took over the priests' houses in those communes which had given up their religion, and used them for works of charity or instruction. It gave a seemingly complacent welcome to the unfrocking of priests and to the anti-religious masquerades which flocked to the bar of the Assembly. During the session of the 30th Brumaire it committed itself still further by admitting a deputation from the "section of Unity," grotesquely attired in priestly garments, and allowing it to defile past with a theatrical parody of Catholic worship. The spokesman of the deputation swore to have no religion but that of Reason, Liberty, Equality and the Republic, and the mob and the members of the Convention shouted, according to the official report: "We swear it! Long live the Republic!"

The Commune of Paris was thus emboldened to kick over the traces, if one may say so, and on the 3rd Frimaire of the Year II. (24th November, 1793), on the request of Chaumette, it decreed "that all the churches and chapels of every religion and sect which exist in Paris shall be closed forthwith," and also that anyone who asked for their reopening should be arrested as a suspicious person.

The Commune was only unconsciously following the example of the municipality of Strasbourg, which on the 2nd Frimaire had ordered the closing of all churches and chapels in the town except those of Reason, and in this they were acting in conformity with a decree passed the day previously by the provisional administrative commission of the Department of the Bas-Rhin.

The Worship of Reason, with its sectional organization in Paris, spread quickly in the departments, through the popular clubs and representatives *en mission*. Many churches were closed and then turned into Temples of Reason. The towns, almost without exception, seemed to rally to this new worship. It was in the south-west especially, and owing to the efforts of the representatives *en mission* Dartigoeyte and Cavaignac, that the movement for the destruction of Christianity became bold even to violence.

Taken as a whole, the tendency of the movement was to substitute what was called natural religion for christianity in any form. Although the Protestants were not unpopular the attitude of some of them in the federalist insurrection had given offence. When they brought their paltry silver church plate these offerings, as we have seen, were accepted after some demurs that were merely formal, but they were accepted all the same. More than one pastor deemed himself bound to resign. The idea of inducing France to become a Protestant nation was foreign both to the revolutionary leaders and to the people at large. Edgar Quinet later on deplored that the scheme had miscarried, for he deemed that protestantizing the country was the true instrument for dethroning Catholicism in it. That which they wanted to set upon the ruins of Christianity was what the philosophers had called natural religion. But which religion? The philosophic sort, according to Voltaire? Or the kind favoured by Rousseau, with Christian formularies? They made no distinction.

Rousseau and Voltaire were both honoured alike. Chaumette, a violent anti-Catholic, posed rather as a disciple of Jean-Jacques Rousseau, while the Voltairian Herbert took pleasure in extolling that "fine sansculotte Jesus." So-called primitive Christianity and natural religion were jumbled up together in the imagination of the Sansculottes, who in 1793 became iconoclasts as much out of patriotism as out of free-thought, and were more concerned at Paris with pulling down than with building up.

The Worship of Reason was nearly everywhere deistic (and not materialistic or atheistic). The popular gatherings for worship in Paris were joyful, full of childish playfulness, in spite of the pedantry of a few learned people. In the provinces the Worship of Reason was taken with more gravity. In the towns, at all events, serious and sincere attempts were made to abolish the old religion and to establish a Worship of Reason. The goddesses of Reason were not actresses, such as they were at Paris, or giddy working girls, but nearly everywhere—and the fact is not denied by the most hostile witnesses—they were lovely young girls, virtuous and serious, the flower of the middle classes.

We are less well informed about the countryside than about the towns. But we know that in the most rural communes many churches were turned into Temples of Reason, and the letters of representatives *en mission* show that the movement towards the overthrow of Christianity spread through almost the whole of France, rural as well as urban.

It is not to be expected that we should find a different aspect or different feelings among the votaries of Reason because they were, for instance, Bretons or Provençals. Philosophic festivals were not publicly celebrated in the same way: the attacks on Christianity were more violent at Strasbourg and at Auch, for instance, than at Chartres and Limoges, for from the summit of the spire of Strasbourg they saw the advanced guards of Austria, at Auch the Revolution was specially threatened by the intrigues of the clergy, while at Chartres the enemy was far away and at Limoges the adversaries of the Revolution were not very dangerous.

The Worship of Reason was also and at the same time the worship of the fatherland, and it was the latter that soon became dominant. Busts of philosophers in the temples were often replaced or flanked by those of Marat, of Chalier, of Le Peletier, who in the fancy of the people personified not mere doctrines, but the France of the Revolution, stabbed in the heart by the dagger of reaction. Gradually the chief honours came to be paid to the three bleeding victims of patriotism.

§ VI

Attitude of the Committee of Public Safety and of the Convention: new proclamation of the liberty of worship

In these circumstances what was the policy of the Government?

It did all it could to oppose violent efforts at destruction and tried, in the midst of all this turbulence, to maintain liberty of worship.

It was not that the members of the Committee of Public Safety desired, as believers, the maintenance of

Catholicism. Everything points to the contrary opinion. They wished and hoped that this religion might disappear gradually as enlightenment gained ground. They did not desire violent persecutions, for they feared that discord would enfeeble the national defence, and they wanted to avoid giving too much scandal to Europe and thus rendering dealings with it impossible.

Robespierre, who at first had kept silence, protested at the Jacobin Club on the 1st Frimaire of the Year II. against the violence of those who would overthrow Christianity. He who was regarded as the head of the Government declared that the Convention, while accepting civic offerings, had not proscribed the Catholic religion and never would take so rash a step; that the intention was to "maintain liberty of worship" and to punish the persecutors of priests. "The man," he said, "who wishes to prevent the saying of Mass is a greater fanatic than he who says it." He denounced those who wished to abolish Christianity as atheists (which was false); he said: "Atheism is aristocratic . . . the idea of a great Being who watches over oppressed innocence and punishes triumphant crime is entirely democratic"; he also denounced the foes of Christianity as traitors and foreign agents: "These cowards would only verify all the gross calumnies which the whole of Europe knows to be impudent falsehoods, and alienate from you, on the ground of religious prejudices and opinions, those whom morality and a common interest would draw towards the sublime cause which we are defending."

Robespierre agreed with Danton when he said, in the Convention, on 6th Frimaire: "I desire that there be no more anti-religious masquerades before the Convention. . . . I demand the erection of the barrier."

This barrier was not, however, set up at once. The Convention continued to receive at its bar the champions of the Worship of Reason, to give honourable mention to letters which announced, in Hébertian style, the resignation of priests, the abuse and destruction of sacred objects, and the inauguration of Temples of Reason. Couthon himself, the follower of Robespierre, brought relics to the Convention and made fun of them. The Convention was represented at the Festival of Reason held on the 10th Frimaire, at Saint-Roch, where the actor Monvel made an Antichristian speech which was reported enthusiastically by the deputation.

But on the 15th Frimaire Robespierre induced the Convention to pass a "Reply to the Manifestos of Kings," in which he denied that the French people had proscribed all religions. "They lie who depict us as a nation of idolaters or madmen." On 16th Frimaire the Convention decreed that "all violence and measures against liberty of worship are forbidden," but the laws against refractory or turbulent priests remained unaltered.

The Commune, on the other hand, was frightened, and had drawn back, declaring, on 8th Frimaire, that, by its decree of the 3rd, it had never "intended to prevent citizens from hiring houses for the exercise of religion, provided that these exercises caused no annoyance to the community." During the winter of 1793-1794 Catholic worship was celebrated in private chapels—notably that of the Oratory, in the Rue d'Enfer, and in that of the Nuns of the Conception, in the Rue Saint-Honoré. They were thronged by the people of Paris and by peasants from the vicinity. These chapels were closed in Floréal of the Year II. by decrees of committees of the sections, and after that it would appear that worship was carried on only in a semi-secret fashion.

§ VII

Dechristianization continues and spreads

The Committee of Public Safety took very seriously the decree of the 16th Frimaire, and did its best to see that representatives *en mission* conformed to it.

Thus, Ingrand complained that he had not been able, in the district of Montmorillon, "to obtain the abjuration of any priest or to reclaim him from his religious follies." The Committee replied on 19th Frimaire: "Let religious ideas alone and they will fall of themselves. It is persecution which gives rise to those horrible wars called sacred." In a circular letter of the 4th Nivôse the Committee said to its representatives: "No doubt the triumph of truth over falsehood is sure; let us hasten it, but do not let us be too precipitate, however grievous it may be to have to contend with opinions which good sense ought to have swept away with the dust of wrecked monarchy. . . . Those whom ancient prejudice still blinds must be enlightened." A blow must be struck at "those scoundrels who preach of heaven the better to devour the earth." Let representatives *en mission* be tolerant towards the former but terrible to conspirators.

Those members of the Committee of Public Safety who went on mission put this counsel into practice.

Jeanbon Saint-André, at Cherbourg, on 21st Frimaire, secured by an order the free exercise of worship, provided that it was confined to places of worship. He said to the inhabitants of the Manche: "Worship the author of Nature in your own way. Jews, Christians, Mohammedans, disciples of Confucius or worshippers of the Grand Lama, you are all equal in the eyes of a free people." The one thing necessary was that no one religion should become predominant.

Some of the representatives on mission continued their violent attacks upon Christianity. Some became moderate. Besides, they met with difficulties in the rural districts. After the middle of November, at Courtalin, in Seine-et-Marne—close to the district whence the first step had been taken to destroy worship—the peasants took up arms in order to claim the reopening of the churches, and Godefroy, the representative *en mission*, advised the Committee of Public Safety to accede to their demand. At Jouy-sur-Morin, in the same department, a hundred men armed with guns, pikes and scythes threatened the representative Morisson, saying that "they wanted the Catholic religion and wanted no more Jacobins." Thus was a religious petition mixed up with a political one. The mixture suggests the question whether, perchance, they were not anti-revolutionists who had stirred up this rising. At Villequiers (Cher) they cried: "We want our religion; we will die to preserve it! We want everything as it used to be and then we will march with a good will." *We want everything as it used to be!* Is it likely that peasants just delivered from the heavy load of feudal rights should ask for the re-establishment of the whole of the old régime? They were more likely repeating, without understanding it, a phrase which had been dictated to them, and their insurrection was inspired by religious motives only.

The churches were not all shut at once and everywhere. In Nivôse of the Year II. churches were open and Catholics were holding services in them in the departments of Dordogne, Loiret and Loir-et-Cher. These variations explain why the anti-revolutionists could not attempt to create agitation everywhere. The injustice of such variations served as an argument to the Catholics of Rouen to obtain, on 27th Frimaire, from the representatives *en mission*, the reopening of all the churches of Rouen. It was the same even in the Marne. These reopenings were almost all only provisional. The churches were closed again in all places where it was observed that gatherings for worship were as much political as religious.

That was the chief reason for the reversal of the decree of 16th Frimaire, which had proclaimed liberty of worship. Revolutionary committees and popular clubs were always declaring to the representatives, and giving proofs for their words, the folly of allowing religous liberty in a time of war at home and abroad, which only served as a mask or a means for anti-revolutionary enterprises. In any case of disturbance, if the representatives probed an inquiry to the bottom, it was seldom that they did not find there the hand of a priest. As troubles and disturbances continued, the movement for the destruction of Christianity also continued strong, even after the institution of the Worship of the Supreme Being—which appeared less Antichristian than the Worship of Reason—and even though more than one Catholic pinned his hopes upon Robespierre. Or, to be more exact, the movement was then at its height. This was the period when the largest number of churches was closed.

In Lot-et-Garonne and the Landes, Monestier, the member for Lozère, although a moderate, made the new Worship of the Supreme Being, which was a development of the Worship of Reason, the dominant and exclusive religion, from the end of Germinal of the Year II. onwards, and thus indirectly abolished Catholicism. Other representatives abolished it by direct means. Siblot, a member of the Convention, having noticed that Mass was still being said in many communes of Seine-Inférieure and Eure, wrote to the Committee: "I put a stop to this by my order of 18th Germinal. There are no more Masses in these two departments, and the people, far from complaining, applauded the measure which they believe will assure peace to them." The representative Vernerey, in Messidor of the Year II., wrote from the Allier: "Before my arrival in this department Roman Catholic worship was carried on openly in nearly every commune. Apostles of Truth and Reason were sent out: they talked to the people with prudence and wisdom, and before I left not a single church remained open. Fanaticism expired without a groan."

One of the most effective measures taken by the Revolution against the Catholic religion was that by which priests, who took part in assemblies prohibited by representatives, could be arrested in the principal town (*chef lieu*) of the district. When there were no more priests there could be no more worship. Sometimes in rural communes the people, who were wedded to their habits, met to sing vespers by themselves, with the schoolmaster in place of the vicar. Even these meetings were forbidden by the Committee of Public Safety as anti-revolutionary —and that in spite of the decree of 16th Frimaire: this was notably the case at Chauny. Writing to Roux, member for the Aisne and the Ardennes, it said: "The Committee beg you to keep a watchful eye upon these treacherous innovations. . . . Disperse these mobs of agitators, smother their dismal croakings; the voice of Reason will succeed in the end, but prudence must prepare its way and assure its victory."

The letters of representatives show that here and there in the country districts there were movements of reaction, even resistance, in favour of Catholicism. Great was the anger, the grief and suffering of pious souls, and in the papers of Robespierre one may read touching laments from Catholics begging him to restore their worship. Among the rebels in La Vendée and Brittany many no doubt took arms from religious motives, or at all events out of love for their priests. But there was no general uprising to demand the restoration of Catholicism, nor even any very large partial rising, such as had been aroused by the question of feudal rights in 1791 and 1792.

No doubt—as I said before with reference to the introduction of the Worship of Reason—we must take account of the fact that the churches were not then all closed at the same time. I said that more were closed afterwards. A memorandum in the papers of Grégoire shows that in Germinal of the Year II. Mass was still being said openly in about a hundred and fifty parishes. We know from trustworthy witnesses that in Thermidor, on the eve of the fall of Robespierre, the Catholic religion was keeping its footing in two districts—namely, Hazebrouck (Nord) and Saint-Hippolyte (Doubs).

I once thought that the conclusion to be drawn from these facts was that the would-be destroyers of Christianity were hurling themselves in vain against a stone wall of moral and material obstacles, and that the attachment of the masses to the Catholic religion, especially in the rural parts, was invincible. From certain instances of resistance and persistence I concluded that this state of mind was general, at any rate among the peasantry. Now, perhaps because I have seen more documents, I am struck by the fewness and slightness of the peasant risings caused by the attacks upon Christianity—and in these risings I note distinctly a mixture of politics with religion.

I am especially impressed by the indifference of the peasant. An example is given by M. L. Testut in his recent history of the little town of Beaumont-du-Périgord. The people of Saint-Avit-Sénieur (Dordogne) wrote to the National Convention towards the end of the Year II.: "For four months past our altars have been without ministers. We should make no complaint if it were not that a part of our taxes is still assigned to the cost of religious worship. It is hard that we should have to go short (for we have nothing to spare) in order to pay for priests who do nothing for us." The writers were middle-class people but they spoke the mind of the peasants. "The peasants," they said, "want their priests because they are paying for them. But if there is anything to be saved by doing without them, you may be sure that they will act according to self-interest, and will perhaps find it convenient not to have any."

§ VIII

Christianity in dire peril

The reason why there was no general rising was that the French peasant is at bottom indifferent to religion. To judge by the *laissez-faire* attitude he has adopted, one would say that his Christianity was superficial and, as it were, a new thing superimposed on his old customs. If he was not stirred to the depths of his soul by the insults to Christianity, it must be that Christianity had not gone very deep with him.

If the system of violence and destruction had been carried out to the end, it seems quite possible that a religion which had never taken deep root might have been uprooted from the consciousness of the peasant. In the country districts this would not have implied the success of " natural religion." The peasant, who was at that time quite illiterate, would no doubt have relapsed for a while into his old pre-Christian habits, to the practices of magic and witchcraft, which were absorbed by Christianity.

It does not seem that the foes of religion encountered any serious difficulties in the towns, either among the artisans or the middle classes. In Paris, and a few other towns where there was a large working-class population, the proletariat—the masses—either applauded the anti-religious parades or took part in them with a visible relish for the irreverence. Not a single protest was raised. It was regarded as a good farce, and the profanities of the newspaper called *Le Père Duchesne* were not at all distasteful to the workmen. The ex-nobles—those of them who remained in France—were quite ready to be infidels, Voltairians. When it was too late, and then for merely political reasons, they made a show of resentment. The middle classes were largely imbued with natural religion of the Voltairian or Rousseau brand—especially the latter. It is quite possible that the scandal caused by the popular insults to the old religion may not have been to their liking, but if so we know nothing about it. We must not forget that the Convention itself—as may be seen in its official reports—applauded these insults, and that Robespierre and Danton dared not oppose them except on political and worldly grounds. Not a single member of the Convention (except Grégoire) dared openly to defend the religion which only the day before had been the religion of the nation.

The Press, if not really free, was not yet the slave which it became after the execution of the Hébertists and Dantonists. A journalist would not have hesitated to criticize the attack on Christianity, all the more so because he knew that his views reflected the secret or avowed opinion of the Government. The only difference between the newspapers was the degree of prominence they gave to accounts of anti-religious manifestations. There was no Press campaign against dechristianization. For in fact this Antichristian movement was, in its inception, mainly a means or expedient of national defence, the defence of the Revolution. Altars were overturned in order to destroy the power of the unpatriotic priests, or (and it comes to the same thing) of anti-revolutionary priests. But patriotism inspired philosophy, as philosophy in its turn inspired patriotism. If the educated Frenchmen of the time had not been ardently patriotic they would not have been so strongly opposed to the Catholic religion. But if they had not been ardently philosophical they would not have pushed the movement of destruction so far, they would not have created such an atmosphere of militant joy.

Patriotism, philosophy and the indifference of the rural masses—these were the causes which gave pause to Christianity. Would they have been finally successful if violence and destruction had continued? One thing is certain, that at the said period the greater part of the French nation had managed to do without religion, the habit of centuries had been broken; and if the historian had bent however keen an ear, no general groan, no great popular wail of grief and anguish, would have been audible to him. If the victories which saved France, which reduced to impotence alike the foreign foe and the anti-revolutionaries whose accomplices the priests seemed to be —if these victories had been long delayed, if patriotism had been the stay of philosophy for a longer period, if there had been any reason for the continuance of violence, who can say that such a course of events might not have proved fatal to Christianity in France?

§ IX

The Worship of the Supreme Being; Robespierre

But let us return to facts. There was one to which I have only alluded—namely, the establishment of the Worship of the Supreme Being, under which the attacks on Christianity went on and which was in truth only the continuation of the Worship of Reason under another form—the form initiated by Robespierre.

Robespierre, an admirer, almost a worshipper, of Jean-Jacques Rousseau, borrowed from him not only his new and eloquent code of morality and his amiable advice about a return to nature—most of his contemporaries did as much—but especially his political-religious views. In his *Social Contract*, Rousseau, while declaring that there must be no "exclusive national religion," pleaded for a "profession of civic faith," which was really nothing but a State religion. He said: "It pertains to the sovereign power (that is, the people) to determine the Articles of their faith, not with the rigidity of religious dogmas, but as social sentiments without which it is not possible to be either a good citizen or a loyal subject." These indispensable doctrines were: the existence of a Divinity at once powerful, intelligent, beneficent, foreseeing and provident, a future life, the happiness of the good, the punishment of the wicked, the sanctity of the social contract and of the laws. You may believe in them or not as you like. If you do not believe you will be banished, not for irreligion, but for lack of social sentiment.

This was Rousseau's idea of the Worship of the Supreme Being, which, following his example, many Frenchmen had adopted inwardly, and in which they found a rule of life. This was the worship which Robespierre desired to make into the State religion and to be himself the pontiff of it. He was waiting for the realization of his plans until the scaffold had rid him of his opponents both of the Right and Left—of the Dantonists, whom he guillotined as traitors for their clemency, the Hébertists, whom he guillotined as traitors for their atheism—including them all in a general accusation of impiety. Then he induced the Committee of Public Safety to adopt his great political-religious scheme, which he himself brought before the National Convention on 18th Floréal of the Year II.

In introducing the scheme he accommodated the ideas of Rousseau to existing circumstances. He fulminated against the men who, having sold themselves to the enemy, "were violently attacking religion in order to become themselves stormy apostles of negation and fanatical missionaries of atheism." He said that he was not denouncing atheism as a philosopher, but as a politician: "To the legislator anything that is of practical utility to the world is true. The idea of the Supreme Being and the immortality of the soul is a continual reminder of justice: therefore it is social and republican." Deism was the religion of Socrates and Leonidas, "and it is a far cry from Socrates to Chaumette and from Leonidas to the newspaper called *Le Père Duchesne*." According to him conspirators have all been atheists, and he denounced as atheists his murdered enemies Gaudet,

Hébert, Vergniaud, Gensonné, Danton. He launched the preacher's anathema against the "sect" of the encyclopædists. After having lauded Rousseau in the tone in which Lucretius extolled Epicurus, he turned on the priests, and in a manner which betrayed irritation, while it expressed reassurance, he contrasted their corrupt Christianity with the purged Christianity of the true servants of the Supreme Being. This Deistical religion ought to be national, and it would be so if all public instruction were directed to the same religious end, and especially if the Divine Being were glorified in popular and official festivals. This religion would prosper if the women wanted it: "O women of France, cherish liberty . . . make use of your power to spread the power of republican virtue."

But was a man free to be a philosopher after the fashion of Diderot for instance? The reply was vague but terrible: "Woe to him who tries to quench sublime enthusiasm!" The new national religion will leave men free only to do good. "Lead us on to victory," said Robespierre, "but before all things hurl vice back into nothingness. The enemies of the Republic are the men who are corrupt." By vice he meant atheism, and all were atheists in religion (and politics too) who did not think like Robespierre. So under this pontificate there would be no more religious liberty.

During the sitting of 18th Floréal of the Year II. (7th May 1794) the decree was passed by which the Worship of the Supreme Being was established and organized.

The first three clauses dealt with its establishment:

"(1) The French people recognize the existence of the Supreme Being and the immortality of the soul; (2) They declare that the best service of the Supreme Being is the practice of the duties of man; (3) In the first rank of those duties they place hatred of treachery and tyranny, the punishment of tyrants and traitors, succour of the unfortunate, respect for the weak, defence of the oppressed, doing all the good one can and not being unjust to anyone." Its organization was the subject of the clauses which instituted festivals "to recall men to the thought of the Divine Being and to the dignity of their own existence." Besides the four political festivals of 14th July 1789, 10th August 1792, 21st January 1793 and of 31st May 1793, there were to be thirty-six other festivals, which should take their names "from the virtues most dear and useful to man, and from the great blessings of nature." At the head of the list came the festival "of the Supreme Being and of Nature"; later on the name of Nature disappeared from this festival, and it was decided in the same decree that, on the 20th Prairial following, the first festival in honour of the Supreme Being should be celebrated by itself.

Before the vote was taken, and when the impression made by the report was under discussion, Couthon said that such an ordinary honour was not enough, that "Providence had been offended," and that they must confer on it the extraordinary honour of a placard in the streets with a translation "into every language."

On the 23rd Floréal the Committee of Public Safety passed a resolution that on the fronts of buildings formerly dedicated to the Worship of Reason the words "*Temple of*

Reason" should be replaced by "*The French people recognize the existence of the Supreme Being and the immortality of the soul*," and that for a month national agents should read to the people in the temples the report and the decree every tenth day. This decree seems to have been carried out everywhere. The new inscription was often engraved in letters of gold. A petition was made that this worship should be subsidized by the State.

The Robespierrist Mayor of Paris, Fleuriot-Lescot, announced in a proclamation to the people of Paris that God would reward France for the decree of 18th Floréal. "Abundance is at hand," he said; "it waits for you. The Supreme Being, protector of the liberty of peoples, has commanded Nature to prepare a plentiful harvest. His eye is upon you: be worthy of His benefits."

The adhesion of the Jacobins was less easy to obtain. The young Jullien, member of the Commission of Public Instruction, and as such a member of the Government, stated at the club that religious sentiment was the soul of patriotism, and that the soldiers sent against the Vendeans were killed only "to take flight to the bosom of the Divinity." The Jacobins hesitated. A lively debate ensued. Robespierre and Couthon had to intervene and evoke the spectre of "foreign conspiracy." Robespierre had even to disavow and secure the rejection of a passage in the address proposed by Jullien in which he demanded, after the fashion of Rousseau, that those who disbelieved in the existence of God should be banished from the Republic. With this amendment the address was adopted. But the secret discontent of the Jacobins was soon expressed by the election of Fouché as president of their club, on the 18th Prairial following, two days before the Festival of the Supreme Being.

When the address was read to the Convention, Carnot, who presided, replied coldly, speaking rather as a disciple of Diderot and seeming to confuse God with Nature; by his choice of words he showed, as plainly as he dared, without running the risk of the guillotine, that he was not at heart attached to the new religion, nor to the pontificate of Robespierre.

Opposition was only timid and cautious. Something happened which allowed Robespierre to take no notice of it. On the 4th Prairial a young girl, Cécil Renault, was arrested on suspicion of wishing to assassinate him; he now posed as a martyr, the martyr of the new religion. A movement of sympathy was immediately felt for Robespierre in many parts of France, and letters have been found among his papers in which he was regarded, not as a mere pontiff, but as a divinity. Deputations crowded to the bar of the Convention to thank the Supreme Being for having saved Robespierre.

On the 16th Prairial he was elected President of the Convention for a fortnight, thereby being appointed in advance to the chief part in the festival of the 20th. The festival took place under his presidency. It was a beautiful one, prepared and staged by David (the great painter and a member of the Convention), quite as imposing as Catholic festivals but in a totally different way. Robespierre made speeches, he set fire to a statue of Atheism, he spoke noble words accompanied by noble gestures. The public did not hear the threatening sarcasms muttered against him by his colleagues who followed behind him. The man stood forth in his glory, he appeared as a leader of the Government and as a religious leader, at once a pontiff and a dictator.

The Worship of the Supreme Being seems, in the retrospect, to have been a reaction against the Worship of Reason on the part of the people as well as of the officials. It is said that some ignorant Catholics were taken in by it and saw in it the first step towards a return to Catholicism. The Abbé Grégoire declares that old women came to these ceremonies holding their missals. But the feeling was not general among the French masses. In spite of the change of inscription on the temples, and of the transformation of the Worship of Reason into the Worship of the Supreme Being, to the militant patriots, to the Sansculottes, especially in the departments, it meant one thing—the destruction and replacement of Catholicism. Before the decree of the 18th Floréal, in worshipping Reason they boasted of worshipping God; after the decree, when worshipping God, they believed themselves to be still adoring Reason—since the one was regarded as an emanation from the other—and we have seen that the work of destroying Christianity went on apace. In reality there was no profound change in the new national and philosophic worship which had been installed in the place of Catholicism—nay, in its own temples. It was the fatherland that was worshipped more and more, whether under the name of Supreme Being or of Reason, and very soon the two cults, which the people could not distinguish one from another, became lost and merged in patriotism.

Patriotism, which was so fervent and religious while

the nation was in danger, was less fervent and less religious when the victory of Fleurus had secured the independence of France. Once the nation was reassured and calmed, the fire of patriotism—which had inspired the Worship of the Supreme Being—burned low, especially after the removal of its pontiff.

CHAPTER IV

CHAPTER IV

THE SEPARATION OF CHURCH AND STATE, 1794–1802

§ I

On September 1794 *the salary of the clergy was stopped*

THE Civil Constitution of the clergy had not been formally abolished, even when Christianity had seemed to be defeated. The salaries of Catholic priests were paid more or less regularly whether they remained at their posts or not. The idea of stopping these salaries had been mooted more than once in the newspapers, the clubs, and even at the rostrum of the Convention, but (as we have seen) without success.

It seemed indeed, when the Terror had been overcome by military victories, that the union of Church and State had become impossible because of the anti-revolutionary attitude taken up by the clergy in general—even by the Constitutional clergy. It seemed also that, as violence was relaxed, it was no longer possible to destroy Christianity by force. The Republic was no longer in danger and things were about to become normal. The decree of the 16th Frimaire of the Year II., which had proclaimed liberty of worship, had not been repealed, though it was violated almost in every direction. In short, the idea of the secularized State had been taught by experience, and therefore people's minds were prepared for separation.

On the 2nd *sans-culottide* of the Year II. (18th September 1794) Cambon proposed, in the name of the Finance Committee, the omission from the budget of the sums for public worship: he had done the same thing in November 1792, but the time was now more opportune. He spoke as a financier but also, in rough and scornful wise, as a philosopher and politician. He showed that the State ought to be independent of all religion. If, he said, the State proclaims any religious principle whatever, there will immediately be a clergy to pay. Had not the ministers of the Cult of the Supreme Being already demanded salaries?

Cambon's motion was forthwith carried with applause.

The principle was "The French Republic will no longer pay the expenses of any religion nor the stipends of its ministers." There followed some temporary arrangements: priests on actual service were allowed the same annual sum that was granted to those who had renounced their orders.

This decree, if one may judge by the terms of the report, was not inspired either by good will towards Catholicism or even by a spirit of liberty. It is quite possible that Cambon saw nothing in it but what he professed to see—namely, a measure of economy—and that it was passed by the Convention only as an act of hostility towards the Church. All the same it seems to have been generally interpreted as a measure of neutrality in regard to Christianity, and, if not a beginning of liberty, at least as a hope of liberty.

But the work of secularization went on. Thus on the 3rd Frimaire of the Year III., at Albi, Mallarmé and Brouillerot, representatives *en mission*, prohibited all exercise of public worship within the district, and all meetings except to celebrate the *décadi*: "If," they declared, "any meeting of citizens takes place under pretence of religious worship, whether in their own houses or anywhere else, such persons shall be declared suspect, and treated as such." No doubt this terrorist proclamation was the result of disturbances; but its terms showed that the zeal of its authors was philosophic as much as patriotic.

On the 27th Brumaire of the Year III., on the report of Lakanal, the Convention had voted for what we should call to-day the secularization of elementary education: religion was banished from the schools and replaced by a study of the Declaration of Rights, of the Constitution and of "Republican morals." Priests' dwellings not already sold were to serve as houses for teachers.

It had proved impossible to destroy Christianity by force, and it therefore became an avowed part of the official programme to destroy it by means of education, the diffusion of light, and by patriotism itself.

This motive underlay the report made on the 1st Nivôse of the Year III., in the name of the Committee of Public Instruction, by Marie-Joseph Chénier, on the organization of those *fêtes décadaires* which had long been under discussion. Chénier believed that prejudice and fanaticism (meaning Christianity, or at all events Catholicism) cannot be destroyed except by way of institutions and instruction, and he proposed to institute a civic festival every tenth day (*décadi*) in all the communes of the Republic: there would be instruction in morals, patriotic songs, and people would dance and enjoy themselves "spontaneously." The Convention voted one of the articles of this project.

During the debate on this question a striking incident occurred. Grégoire, member of the Convention and

Constitutional bishop, appeared on the tribune in sacerdotal garb and made a long speech, in which he demanded liberty of worship, and in which he contrasted the Christian with the philosophic spirit, called aloud for the revival of Catholicism, and insinuated that in his opinion the Republic's only chance of life was to become Christian. The Convention set to work keenly upon "the order of the day," on the motion of Grégoire.

This speech made a great impression, and was the signal for the restoration of Catholicism which was almost spontaneous.

In Loir-et-Cher, Grégoire's own diocese, the churches reopened on the 1st January 1795 and the Constitutional clergy returned to their duties. Elsewhere, in the Department of the Doubs, it was the non-juring clergy who set up the altars. In Brittany and in La Vendée religion was re-established by representatives *en mission*, members of the Committee of Public Safety. This movement of religious resurrection spread. Moreover, this was the time when the Convention began the negotiations which resulted in the treaties of Bâle, and, as in the time of Robespierre, it was determined not to seem atheistical or even irreligious.

§ II

Law of 3rd Ventôse, Year III.; separation and liberty; re-establishment of the Constitutional Church and re-appearance of the Catholic worship

For these reasons some degree of legal freedom was restored to Catholicism by the decree of the 3rd Ventôse of the Year III. (21st February 1795) on the report of Boissy d'Anglas.

He rejoiced in the separation. "Citizens," he said, "public worship has been banished from the Government and it will not return." Then he declared the Catholic religion to be intolerant, domineering, sanguinary, childish, absurd and harmful. The ideal would be that instead of religion men should be led by the light of reason and bound to each other by ties of mere common interest, by the principles of social organization, and by that imperious feeling which draws men to gather together and to love one another. It was by "the wisdom of the laws" that the Convention would prepare for "the sole reign of philosophy, for the sway of morality alone. . . . Absurd dogmas will be no sooner recognized than despised. Very soon the religion of Socrates and of Marcus Aurelius and of Cicero will be the religion of the world." But to attain this end we must go slowly, like nature. Let there be no Hébertism, no persecution.

Thus the plan of substituting natural religion for Christianity was reaffirmed. Christianity could not be overthrown by violence. They hoped to do it by liberty —and strict legal restraints.

This law of the 3rd Ventôse of the Year III. proclaimed liberty for all religions, condemned as misdemeanants those who opposed or insulted the exercise of public worship, declared that the State would not give pay to any priest or provide any building for worship, prohibited all external ceremonies, signs or inscriptions and all public proclamations or calling of assemblies. No one might appear in public in canonicals or wear ornaments used in religious ceremonies. All religious gatherings were placed under police supervision. The communes were not to acquire nor let any place for religious purposes. No endowment, either permanent or temporary, might be created, nor might any tax be imposed for the maintenance of religion.

Catholicism immediately reappeared everywhere, both in Paris and in the departments, with a spontaneous revival, in which both sections of the clergy took part, the non-jurors and the Constitutional clergy.

The non-jurors who had emigrated returned stealthily one by one. They were richer and more zealous than the Constitutionals. They took their orders from the Pope, several of them came from Rome. Others who till then had been lurking in safe hiding-places reappeared in public.

The legal existence of the Constitutional clergy came to an end. But the good will of the authorities was on their side, especially as many of the non-juring priests were still under the ban of the proscription laws. Municipal officers and representatives *en mission* attended Masses said by Constitutional priests.

At first these former official clergy were rather embarrassed by the advantages which the non-jurors got out of the law of the 3rd Ventôse. But Grégoire consoled and, in truth, organized them. He was the first person who dared to reassume episcopal functions. On the 22nd Ventôse in the Year III. he addressed a pastoral letter to his diocese, which made a great stir and had a great result, because he announced the reconciliation of the Revolution and Christianity. "The vessel of the Republic," he said, "and that of the Church, battered by storms, will now sail side by side and arrive happily in port."

Three days later, on the 25th Ventôse, the Constitutional bishops who met at Paris addressed an encyclical "to their brothers the other bishops and to the vacant churches." They congratulated themselves on the separation of Church and State. They reorganized the Gallican Church, arranged for the election of the bishops and their institution by their colleagues, and preserved the ecclesiastical districts and parishes of 1790. It was the Civil Constitution, but without the claims and the support of the State. These bishops founded a Christian philosophical society composed of clergy and laity of which Grégoire was the soul. They started a periodical called *Annales de la Religion*. Some months later they published a new encyclical which contained "regulations for the re-establishment of the Gallican Church." It was therein stated that "the Government of the Christian Republic is not monarchic: authority rests with the bishops, who are the successors of the apostles." They declared their attachment to the four Articles of 1682 and convoked a National Council for the 1st May 1796.

The Constitutional Church was therefore revived and living, but it was poor; it was not so easy for it as it had been for the non-jurors to find chapels and houses. When General Hoche, in Brittany, invited the Constitutional Bishop Lecoz to preach to the rustics the bishop replied: "Where will they meet if they have no churches?" There was soon a universal stir, and on every side a cry went up for the restoration of the churches.

§ III

Law of 11th Prairial, Year III.: restitution of the churches to the faithful

On the 11th Prairial of the Year III. Lanjuinais, in the name of the Government Committees, drew up a report in which he showed that the restoration of churches to the faithful would reconcile them to the Republic. He said that "the impossibility of watching over assemblies in private houses, and the ease with which fanaticism and rebellion might be encouraged in such assemblies, ought to suffice to make the Convention permit the use of churches." But he required that ministers of religion should make a declaration of submission to the laws of the Republic. A decree to this effect was passed during the sitting. Citizens were provisionally allowed the free use of the churches which had not been alienated, provided they maintained them and kept them in repair. When inhabitants of the same commune, or section of a commune, professed different religions, or so-called religions, and they all claimed the use of the same building, it should be granted to them in common, and the municipal authorities, under the superintendence of the *corps administratif*, should fix the days and hours convenient for each religion, and also the measures for the preservation of decent behaviour, peace and concord. Ministers who exercised their functions without having made this declaration were punishable by a fine of a thousand francs.

This decree of the 11th Prairial restored twelve churches in Paris to the uses of religion—that is, one for each arrondissement. This number was subsequently increased to fifteen. On the 24th Thermidor (11th August 1795) the keys of Notre-Dame were delivered to a "Catholic Society" composed of Grégoire, Agier, Royer, Saurine, and many members of the former Constitutional clergy. Four days later the Feast of the Assumption was celebrated there by the Society, and after sharing the church for some time with the *théophilanthropes* they continued to use it till the Concordat, when Bonaparte turned them out. Similar societies were organized in many places in the departments.

On the 26th Prairial of the Year III. it was announced by a circular of the Legislative Committee that the declaration of submission to the laws of the Republic was not retrospective, that the Civil Constitution of the clergy was abolished, and that therefore the churches were restored equally to those who had not accepted this Constitution and to those who had.

How far did the non-juring clergy profit by the permission? Details are lacking. It is scarcely likely that in the then state of opinion they were able to obtain and make use of many churches, especially as we may suppose that they would object to sharing them. They were content, no doubt, almost everywhere, with the same chapels and the same houses as before. But they came out into the open and manifested the zeal which the new law allowed.

Popular sympathy was on the side of the clergy who had remained faithful to the Pope, especially in the country districts, and this not because of their fidelity, but because they were the old clergy, while the ex-Constitutional clergy found clients among the middle classes and the inhabitants of towns—or, I should say, among a part of them.

The revival of the Catholic religion was even favoured by the rivalry of the two sects and, under the auspices of Gallicans and Ultramontanes, a great part of the nation returned to its habits of worship. Soon after the fall of Robespierre the Protestants had resumed their worship, at any rate in Paris. As soon as Pastor Marron was set at liberty he officiated at the Temple of Saint-Louis. Protestants increased under the Revolution; the Consistory soon had to hire another church, a *dépendance* of the ex-convent of the Visitation of the Daughters of Sainte-Mary.

§ IV

Law of 7 Vendémiaire, Year IV.; general regulation of worship

On the 7th Vendémiaire of the Year IV. (29th September 1795) the Convention passed an important law on the general organization of religion, by which previous laws were amalgamated into one.

This law proclaimed anew the principle of liberty and separation. It fixed the formula of submission. "I recognize the supremacy of the body of French citizens and I promise submission and obedience to the laws of the Republic." The dominance of any one religion was provided against. No ceremony might take place outside the permitted churches except in private houses, and provided that not more than ten people were present. (This clause was directed against the "refractory" clergy, who were suspected of anti-revolutionary plots in their meetings.)

The other principal regulations were: (1) no writing might be published which came from a minister of religion residing out of France; (2) perpetual imprisonment for any minister inciting to the re-establishment of the monarchy or other anti-revolutionary acts; (3) two years imprisonment for any minister who spoke against the sale of national property.

The law was the creature of circumstance drawn up on the morrow of a civil war; it was also a police law, but it was above all a law of liberty.

It allowed the general revival of Catholicism, which for a moment seemed to have been swept away by violence among a people who possessed a minority of unbelievers, another minority of believers and a mass of indifferents.

The former Constitutional clergy used their new liberty while adhering to the Republic which had given them back their churches. The refractory clergy also took advantage of it, but often in order to preach revolt. Emigrant priests returned in crowds. That was why, on the 3rd Brumaire of the Year IV., the Convention ordered that the laws of 1792 and 1793 against priests subject to deportation and confinement should be enforced within twenty-four hours, at the same time annulling those proclamations of its committees and representatives *en mission* which were contrary to these laws. It aimed at seditious persons, not as priests, but as citizens. Religious liberty was maintained for all who submitted to the laws.

Thus was instituted the régime which we call the Separation of Church and State, defined in these terms by the Constitution of the Year III., Article 354: "No one can be prevented from exercising, conformably to the laws, the religion of his choice. No one can be forced to contribute to the expenses of a religion. The Republic pays no stipends." This régime lasted until the Concordat came into force in 1802—that is, for seven years.

I have sketched elsewhere (in my *Political History of the Revolution* and in my *Studies and Lessons*) the history of these seven years of the Separation of Church and State. Many historians see in it only persecutions on the part of the executive of the Directory—which was more anti-clerical than the Convention, and it is a well-known fact that the Directory deported numbers of refractory priests suspected of being anti-revolutionaries, especially after the *coup d'état* of the 18th Fructidor of the Year V.

But the system worked. It allowed all the liberty compatible with the circumstances and the passions of a country which had just been distressed by a foreign war and by a civil war which was not yet quite over. Different religions existed side by side; they quarrelled sometimes, but they survived. The people bubbled over with religious life, and philosophy flourished among the elect. There was no dominant religion and no sect succeeded in becoming tyrannical. Just or unjust, legal or dictatorial, the severities of the Directory towards the Catholics, who were the most considerable sect, prevented them from obtaining any preponderance, and a kind of religious equilibrium was established under the superior independence of the State.

§ V

List of religious sects and of rationalist groups under the Separation: religious policy of the Directory; de-christianization under the régime of liberty by means of public instruction and "fêtes décadaires"

The following is a brief summary of religious parties and philosophic and rationalist groups under the system of Separation.

The reorganization of Catholicism with its two parties was quickly accomplished. We read in the *Annales de la Religion* for the 6th Messidor of the Year VI.: "At the beginning of last Vendémiaire—that is, the end of September 1797—a list was made by the Ministry of Finance of all communes which had resumed the public exercises of religion. Nine months ago there were 31,214, whilst another 4511 had applied for leave, and in this calculation Paris was not included; large communes only counted for one church, so that we get almost our 40,000 old parishes."

Thus, two years after the Separation, Catholicism was generally restored in France. We see then that a number of churches have been reopened—almost all the parish churches in fact. It is a question whether they were as well frequented as before the attempt to destroy Christianity. I do not think so, but there are no statistics. What we can say is, that it had now been admitted by law and custom that it was possible to live without religion. It is certain that philosophical unbelief was fashionable in Government circles and that this fashion was spread by almost all the Press organs of the Left. Certainly some people who went to Mass before 1793 had left off going, and these were mainly militant patriots—especially in towns. On the other hand, it appeared, for instance, in the Department of the Sarthe, that many peasants who did not go to church towards the end of the old régime were now beginning to go when the churches were reopened—less, perhaps, from a return to the faith than as a political protest or from force of example. Their number was doubtless not large enough to compensate for the loss of the free-thinkers who were now emboldened by the new laws and new customs.

In these reopened parishes what proportion did the papal party bear to the non-papal? What was the numerical position of the two Catholic parties?

It is impossible to give the numbers of the faithful, but there is every indication that the papal party was much more considerable than the Constitutional. Nevertheless the adherents and the ministers of the Gallican Church, created by the Constitution and given the position of a non-official Church, were numerous enough to make them a serious menace to the Roman Church. We have figures for the episcopate only. A report by Grégoire shows that in the Year V. there remained only forty-one out of eighty-three bishops elected or confirmed in 1790. Out of the forty-two missing nine had married—and so were rejected—six had resigned, six had not resumed their functions, eight had been guillotined, thirteen had died a natural death. Three vacant sees—Colmar, Versailles and Saint-Omer—had been filled. Most sees were therefore occupied, and it might be said that the Constitutional Church was reorganized.

At first, the vessels of the Republic and of the Church had kept company, according to Grégoire's prediction. But this harmony was soon broken. The question of the marriage of priests, on which the Constitutional Church was inflexible, and above all the observance of the tenth day (*décadi*), on which it was almost equally intractable, cooled its relations with the State, and this coolness became almost a rupture after the *coup d'état* of the 18th Fructidor of the Year V.

This rupture—or half-rupture—did not prevent the Directory from seeing the advantage of protecting these schismatics against the Pope, and it allowed them to hold synods and a National Council. This Council, at first announced for 1st May 1796, was held at Notre-Dame, in Paris, 15th August 1797 to the 12th November following. It protested that it had had no intention of creating a schism. A bargain was proposed to the Pope under the name of "decree of pacification." The Pope turned a deaf ear. This conciliatory attitude of the Constitutional Church leads us to think that it did not feel it was making headway with the people, or that the number of its adherents was increasing. All the same it continued to exist, it had power, it made a great figure, it prevented the Roman Church from regaining predominance.

The papal party had also lost many of its bishops. Forty-one had died. They had not all emigrated, as is sometimes said; eleven had never quitted France: those of Troyes, Chalon-sur-Saône, Marseilles, Angers, Séez, Senlis, d'Alais, Saint-Papoul, Lectoure, Macon and Sarlat. Of the *émigrés* one at least, d'Aviau, Archbishop of Vienne, returned to France under the Directory. Some absentees tried to rule from a distance. In some dioceses, vacant through the death of the incumbent (Louis XVIII., in the depths of exile, made no appointments), there were apostolic vicars. But we have no materials for even an approximate list of old régime dioceses which were reorganized. And, in spite of imprisonment and deportations, the number of refractory vicars and curates who had returned to the exercise of their functions was large.

If we may judge by Paris, the Roman Church, after the establishment of the Separation, was very flourishing, and it is for Paris that we have most information. At the Easter festival of April 1797 (Germinal, Year V.), if we may rely on one of its ministers, the Abbé de Boulogne, services were held in fifty chapels or churches in Paris. After the 18th Fructidor chapels and oratories were closed by order of the Government. But the papistical clergy had full liberty to celebrate their worship, with large congregations, in the eight churches—Saint-Gervais, Saint-Thomas-d'Aquin, Saint-Philippe-du-Roule, Saint-Laurent, Saint-Eustache, Saint Jacques-du-Haut-Pas, Saint-Roch, Saint-Nicolas-des-Champs. The one thing necessary was that the ministers should take a new oath attesting their hatred of monarchy and anarchy. A portion of the refractory clergy, under the influence of the Abbé Emery, had made this declaration of submission, and the same persons, or nearly so, took the oath of allegiance to the Republic. The many who had not taken it and who nevertheless wished to exercise their functions were arrested.

Little was heard of the other Christians, the two Protestant sects—Calvinists and Lutheran—under the

Separation. The same may be said of the Jews. Both Protestants and Jews submitted to the laws and silently enjoyed the liberty accorded them after centuries of persecution. The Government seems to have had no need to trouble about any of them.

The philosophers and rationalists proceeded with the movement for the abolition of Christianity, in which they had the support of the Government.

The idea of the Directory, at any rate sometimes, was that its part was more than that of umpire in the rivalry of churches. It had a philosophical and political bias against the Roman Catholic Church. The clearest expression of its purpose is found in its letter to General Bonaparte, Commander of the Army in Italy, dated 13 Pluviôse of the Year V. and signed by La Revellière-Lépeaux, Barras and Reubell. They told him that "the Roman religion would always be the irreconcilable enemy of the Republic." It must be struck in France; it must be struck in Rome. "There are, no doubt," they said, "means which can be employed at home to diminish its influence insensibly, either by legislation or by institutions which will efface old impressions by substituting new ones more agreeable to the actual order of things, more conformable to reason and a sound morality. But there is one thing even more essential to the attainment of the end desired, and that is to destroy, if possible, the centre of unity of the Roman Church; and it is for you, who unite in your person the most distinguished qualities of the general and of the enlightened politician, to realize this aim if you consider it practicable."

This was the moment when the victories of the Army

in Italy appeared to place the Pope at the mercy of the French Government.

At home the policy of the Directory tended to eliminate revealed religion little by little from the national conscience by educating that conscience, not only by way of secular public instruction, but by the organization of civic festivals to celebrate the *culte décadaire*, which was to be a national religion, like the Worship of the Supreme Being, but freely exercised with the co-operation of the private sects.

The Convention before dispersing had organized festivals to be celebrated every tenth day (*décadi*). These had been fairly well observed before the 18th Fructidor, but it was only after the *coup d'état* that the *culte décadaire* was made compulsory and endowed with the same character of a State religion as the Cult of the Supreme Being. It was still patriotism under the semblance of religion, the patriotism to which altars had been reared spontaneously in 1790 in the popular movement of the federations, a movement which had grown cold when the country had ceased to be in danger; it was this movement which the Directory was trying to restore, especially as a check to Catholicism.

One of its means was the issue of proclamations and laws for the strict observance of the Republican Calendar, which absolutely excluded the use of the old Christian Calendar, which might not even be employed concurrently with the other. The tenth day (*décadi*) was endowed with all the privileges of Sunday, and any cessation of work on Sundays was forbidden.

As to civic festivals, in every canton, every tenth day

(*décadi*), according to the law of the 13th Fructidor of the Year VI., the municipal administration, the commissioner of the Directory and the secretary, standing before the altar of the "fatherland," erected generally in the parish church, or "other place proper to meetings of citizens," had to read the laws and acts of authority from a "*décadaire bulletin* of the general affairs of the Republic," which also contained articles on civics and virtue, and instruction in agriculture and the mechanical arts. Marriages might be solemnized only on the *décadi*, and in the same place. The masters and mistresses of schools, whether public or private, were bound to bring their pupils. The *décadi* was also celebrated by games and gymnastics. As a matter of fact, and in spite of its obstinate zeal, the Directory had great trouble in getting the *décadi* observed. The old Constitutional clergy manifested almost as much dislike to it as the papist clergy, and if they submitted it was not with a good grace. The quarrel between Monsieur Dimanche and Citizen Décadi, as the pamphlets said, resulted in complete victory for neither. The peasants had got the Sunday habit, and they held to it more firmly perhaps than their priests. It seems to have been found impossible in rural France to substitute the rest of the *décadi* for the Sunday rest. The result was that in many places the peasants observed them both.

In the parish churches the worship of the *décadi* was carried on side by side with the other cults. Thus a proclamation of the Central Administration of the Seine stated that each of the twelve municipalities of Paris should celebrate the *décadis* in one of the fifteen churches restored to the use of the citizens. The services of other religions must be over before half-past eight on the morning of the *décadi* and might not be resumed till the services of the *décadi* were over. The symbols of other religions must be covered up or taken away during the performance of the *décadi* functions. Thus the worship of the tenth day (*décadi*) assumed the appearance of the dominant cult in all buildings, and in some towns the churches were even deprived of their Christian appellations. For instance, by a proclamation of the Central Administration of the Seine, issued on the 22nd Vendémiaire of the Year VI., Saint-Philippe-du-Roule became the Temple of Concord, Saint-Roch the Temple of Genius, Saint Eustache the Temple of Agriculture, Saint Germain-l'Auxerrois the Temple of Gratitude, Saint-Laurent the Temple of Old Age, Saint-Nicolas-des-Champs the Temple of Hymen, Saint-Merry the Temple of Commerce, Sainte-Marguerite the Temple of Liberty and Equality, Saint-Gervais the Temple of Youth, Notre-Dame the Temple of the Supreme Being, Saint Thomas-d'Aquin the Temple of Peace, Saint-Sulpice the Temple of Victory, Saint-Jacques-du-Haut-Pas the Temple of Beneficence, Saint-Médard the Temple of Work, Saint-Étienne-du-Mont the Temple of Filial Duty. The external characteristics of the churches were thus dechristianized, and the public were indifferent, or at least no general protest was raised.

As a rule the services of the tenth day (*fêtes décadaires*) were observed with more curiosity than zeal. Congregations were thin, except at weddings, which were performed free of charge in some places—to the loss of the Catholic religion. At the end of Vendémiaire in the Year VII. the commissioner of the Directory in the neighbourhood of the Central Administration of the Seine noted that in the canton of Pierrefitte "the services of the tenth day (*décadi*) were so gaining ground that marriages solemnized according to the new rites were no longer submitted to the *visa* of the vicar."

This civil religion, this religion of patriotism officially imposed, and itself a pale reflection of the Cult of the Supreme Being, was not popular. Nevertheless its ceremonies, frigid as they were, found their way into the life of the people, at any rate in Paris. The civic altars of the fatherland, set up in the churches, recalled the great attempt to dethrone Christianity. They were, when Bonaparte suppressed them in 1802, one of the visible signs of secularization, a symbol, a suggestion, an official expression of a State philosophy.

Another reflection or consequence of the Cult of the Supreme Being was Theophilanthropy, founded by certain private persons belonging to the cultured middle class, in Nivôse of the Year V., in Paris. It was a "natural religion," not at all that of Rousseau and Robespierre, which was a purged and primitive sort of Christianity, but rather that of Voltaire and the English free-thinkers, whose tenets were pre-Christian and superior to it. Its members were Deists, but tolerant, sufficiently so to admit an atheist like Sylvain Maréchal. They had no use for revelation or mystical dogmas. Their worship, which might take place at home or in temples, consisted in gatherings for mutual encouragement in morality. They had no ceremonies, only a few moral inscriptions and a simple altar decked with fruit and flowers. They sang hymns and honoured the heroes of humanity: Socrates, Saint-Vincent-de-Paul, Jean-Jacques Rousseau and Washington.

This cult, founded by the bookseller Chemin, and protected by La Reveillière-Lépeaux, a member of the Directory, was never popular, but it included many of the élite among politicians, literary men and artists, such as Dupont (of Nemours), Bernardin de Saint-Pierre, Marie-Joseph Chénier, Andrieux, and the painter David.

The Theophilanthropists of Paris enjoyed the use of eighteen chapels or churches. The Directory paid the cost of their installation at Notre-Dame. The Minister of the Interior disseminated the *Manuel* of Chemin in the departments post free and under his private seal. The jury of instruction gave official approval to their catechism, which thus became a classic. Nevertheless Theophilanthropy did not become a State religion, like the *culte décadaire*, although a motion to that effect was brought forward at the Council of Five Hundred on the 9th Fructidor of the Year V. As the religion of an aristocracy of intellect it could not expect many adherents. But it persisted, it had its devotees and was one of the obstacles to the preponderance of Roman Catholicism when Bonaparte abolished it in 1802.

Side by side with or above these rationalist cults stood free-thought, with an official organization in the heart of the National Institute, where the classes in moral and political science included the foremost free-thinkers of the time—Volney, Garat, Ginguené, Cabanis, Lakanal, Naigeon. Their organ, the *Décade philosophique*, was an important review. From this lofty centre radiated a philosophic spirit, Antichristian certainly, but peaceful, and making no appeal to violence.

§ VI

General secularization: destruction of the whole régime by the Concordat

Such is, in short, the list of religious and philosophical organizations under the system of Separation.

If the Directory failed to realize its design, half secret and half avowed, of destroying the Catholic religion, its policy had popularized the idea of the Secular State and strengthened the secular character which the State already possessed by its Constitution. It made sure that public instruction should be placed on a purely rationalist basis. In a circular to the teachers of central schools on 17th Vendémiaire of the Year VII., François de Neufchâteau, Minister of the Interior, ordered them to remove from their teaching "everything that pertained to the doctrines and rites of all religions and sects whatever they might be." Nothing must be taught but "universal morality." After the 18th Fructidor the Directory required candidates for public offices to have attended the schools of the State. A strict inspection of free schools was organized, with intent to close all those in which the teaching was not founded on the rationalist principles of the French Revolution.

Such was the politico-religious régime which Bonaparte destroyed in 1802 after concluding a concordat with Pope Pius VII.

It is often said that he raised up the altars anew.

That is not the case. They were raised up everywhere, and religious as well as philosophic life was flourishing. On the contrary, he overthrew the altars, those of the Constitutional Church, of the *culte décadaire*, of the Theophilanthropists. He crushed the free-thinkers of the Institute by suppressing the classes in moral science and scattering the members through the other classes. This secularity of the State, which was so firmly established by the Directory, was altered by Bonaparte in favour of the Roman Church. He strengthened the Church by putting an end to the Constitutionalist schism. He discredited militant free-thought and rendered it almost inoffensive. In short, he re-established the Roman Church in its dominant position, not certainly for piety's sake, but for policy. He thought that he was going to dominate the Pope, and through the Pope the consciences of mankind.

INDEX

INDEX

INDEX

INDEX

INDEX